imagination @work

SHIFTING BOUNDARIES IN THE MODERN WORKPLACE

A Collection of Insights from Leading HR and OD Experts

Maria Baker

Michele Fantt Harris

Denise Jerome

Lisa M. Johnson

Michael Rider

Foreword by: Jeff Nally

SILVER TREE PUBLISHING

Imagination@Work: Shifting Boundaries in the Modern Workplace

Published by Silver Tree Publishing, a division of
Silver Tree Communications, LLC (Kenosha, WI).
www.SilverTreePublishing.com

Contributing Authors:
Maria Baker
Michele Fantt Harris
Denise Jerome
Lisa M. Johnson
Michael Rider

Foreword by:
Jeff Nally

Editing by:
Kate Colbert

Cover Design and Typesetting by:
Courtney Hudson

First edition, June 2019

Imagination@Work is the fourth and final volume in the @Work Series from
Silver Tree Publishing, in collaboration with Cathy Fyock, LLC.

ISBN: 978-1-948238-11-3

Library of Congress Control Number: 2019905727

Created in the United States of America

Acknowledgments
from the Publishers

We want to express our gratitude to the five authors who have contributed to this anthology — to Maria Baker, Michele Fantt Harris, Denise Jerome, Lisa M. Johnson and Michael Rider. We value the faith that each author had in us, and cherished the journey we took together. With highly personal stories and insights about leaders and organizations who embodied imagination in the workplace, our amazing authors generously gave us the pleasure of working with them to compile this anthology. We treasure these stories even more because, through the authoring and publishing process, we had the chance to get to know each author as an individual. Their powerful stories, keen insights and important practical advice were universally shared with enthusiasm, professionalism and imagination. It has been a privilege to work with each of them.

We'd like to share a special note of thanks to Jeff Nally for authoring the foreword to this book — for providing contexts for our readers about the importance of this entire volume dedicated to stretching our imaginations in the workplace. His perspectives and sneak-peeks of what await you in the chapters make this book stronger, and will, no doubt, be appreciated by our readers.

This has been the fourth and final anthology in our @Work Series, and we also would like to thank the authors who participated in

Humans@Work, *Compassion@Work* and *You@Work*. Genuine thanks is extended to each of the 50 authors who contributed their insights to these projects.

We're also proud of the many anthology authors who — after experiencing the career and life benefits of co-authoring an anthology — have since written and published solo-authored books. We congratulate them on this bold step in their continuing thought leadership and brand building.

While we are closing out this anthology series with this final remarkable book, we would still like to extend an invitation to aspiring authors who have an interest in participating in an anthology or their own solo book project. We've included additional information at the end of the book about how you can get in touch with us. We'd love to talk with you about how we might support *your* dream of making the workplace and the world a better place, one word at a time.

Kate Colbert, *Silver Tree Publishing*
Cathy Fyock, *The Business Book Strategist*

Table of Contents

Foreword

*"The true sign of intelligence is not knowledge, but imagination." – **Albert Einstein***

If you're like me, just seeing the words "imagination" and "work" in the same sentence strikes you as a contradiction. Organizations are structured for efficiency, filled with hierarchies, and both battered and constrained by boundaries. Where would imagination have any place at work?

As an executive coach, I consistently hear from leaders in organizations that they aren't given much permission, time or freedom to imagine. While corporations and customers clamor for innovation, there's not much room in the day-to-day busy-ness of business for imagination to spark innovation and inspire change.

———————

While corporations and customers clamor for innovation, there's not much room in the day-to-day busy-ness of business for imagination to spark innovation and inspire change.

———————

One executive shared with me, "Our coaching session is the one hour each week during which I get to think clearly, and have new ideas that help me and my team." That got me wondering ... what happens the other 50 or 60 hours of his workweek? *Imagination@Work* is more than a book title for this anthology, but truly a way of thinking, being and leading. It begs the question, about this coaching client and all leaders: What are companies and careers missing when the vast majority of our time at work is devoid of imagination? Moreover, it has me concerned that organizations are creating less room, time or appreciation for employees who are striving to make room for imagination in the workplace. Where will those enterprising and passionate employees go, and what will become of them if they are stifled for too long?

PAGES UPON PAGES OF INSPIRATION

> *"All our dreams can come true, if we have the courage to pursue them."* **– Walt Disney**

Even our daily lives crowd out the time and space for imagination. Our days are filled with logistics, tasks and activities that are keenly focused on the here and now, as we jump from obligation to obligation, meeting to meeting, crisis to crisis, problem to yet another problem, and, yes, email to email to email. The fact of the matter is that we simply don't have many opportunities to imagine what could be, or take the time to spark imagination to create the future we want for ourselves and the people we care about. We're in an imagination-dampening culture. It's time for you to launch into an imagination-inspiring space, and *Imagination@Work* is the book to take you there. Let me tell you what to expect as you turn the following pages — how the five authors of this book will inform, inspire and empower you.

Maria Baker

Instead of making assumptions or falling victim to generalities about millennials, it's time for you to take the mystery out of millennials at work with Maria Baker's chapter, *Welcome Millennials! There's Room for Us All at the Top.* Maria takes you on a fast-track journey into the mind of the millennial and guides all generations at work through the key elements to ensure everyone is successful in the workplace, creates a positive impact on the organization and makes room for every generation at the top.

The fact of the matter is that we simply don't have many opportunities to imagine what could be, or take the time to spark imagination to create the future we want for ourselves and the people we care about. We're in an imagination-dampening culture.

Michele Fantt Harris

Sometimes our imagination is on fire and we just can't stop the new ideas and insights. That's what author Michele Fantt Harris demonstrates in this anthology. Her imagination sparked *two* chapters!

First, she shares a workplace coaching model that anyone can use. It's a simple, yet powerful, way to ignite an employee's imagination to solve a workplace problem or improve performance. Michele shares research that proves the positive impact of asking coaching questions instead defaulting to a command-and-control approach. By the end of her chapter, you'll be ready to start asking questions like a coach.

Next, Michele reimagines the exit interview and inspires you to create stay interviews in her chapter, *Exit Interviews vs. Stay Interviews.* Wouldn't you like to get inside the imagination of current employees and learn what motivates them to keep coming to work? And if an employee decides to leave, imagine how valuable it is to learn what could have been changed or improved to keep that talent from walking out the door.

Michele is an experienced people-practice professional who generously shares the secrets to meaningful exit and stay interviews, so take her advice and put her expertise to work for you!

Denise Jerome

The power of stories lies at the heart of Denise Jerome's chapter, *It All Starts with Your Story*. Denise reminds you that stories aren't just for writers or fictional characters. Using your imagination to create your own story leads to more meaning, purpose, innovation and engagement at work. Denise shows you and your team how to create stories that propel people and organizations into unimaginable success.

Lisa Johnson

Does the word "compliance" make you think of imagination? Well, just wait until you read Lisa Johnson's chapter on *Managing Compliance with Confident Communications*. Lisa shows you how to take the fear out of difficult employee relations situations so you can lead with confidence and communicate with clarity. Lisa is a seasoned human resources professional who has thrived amid tough compliance issues in manufacturing companies, so you can trust her reimagined approach to confident communications.

Michael Rider

Michael Rider's personal story will surprise you and inspire you. And his chapter, *Living an Engaged Life at Work Through Mentoring*, will spark your imagination to bring mentoring to your organization and to the people you care about. Michael shows you how to create a variety of mentor-mentee relationships that will deepen engagement and motivate individuals to live a reimagined life. Michael is a model of authenticity and generosity, so take his chapter to heart and live a more engaged life.

IMAGINE THE PREVIOUSLY IMPOSSIBLE

"I am enough of an artist to draw freely upon my imagination. Imagination is more important than knowledge. Knowledge is limited. Imagination encircles the world." **– Albert Einstein**

You haven't even begun to enjoy the chapters of this book, and yet I am sure you can already tell that a book about embracing imagination in the workplace — about shifting the boundaries that restrain and constrain us — is a book that could not have found an eager audience 25 or 50 years ago. For our parents, grandparents, great-grandparents, work was simply work. It was about production and obligation, about accuracy and reliability and trustworthiness. In all but a few rare and inherently creative professions (like music), it most certainly wasn't about imagination, individuality or innovation.

Maria Montessori, the founder of the Montessori method of childhood education, imagined the impossible during her high school years in the late 1800s. She imagined becoming an engineer, something unheard of for women during her time. And by the time she graduated from college, she re-imagined herself as a physician, the pinnacle role in another male-dominated profession. Montessori said, *"Imagination does not become great until human beings, given the courage and the strength, use it to create."*

Imagination without the courage to act on the insights and ideas that it generates is like a having a faint daydream: it's amusing and distracting, but it won't spark change or action. The authors you're about to experience in *Imagination@Work* are courageous, strong and inspired human beings who, like Montessori, have picked up their big ideas, acted upon them and made a positive, powerful impact on the world at large.

How will *you* spark your imagination? What's your insight that needs to be imagined in new ways? How will you put your imagination to work — this year, this week or even today? Turn the page, learn from these imaginative authors, and let's experience your *Imagination@Work*.

Jeff Nally, PCC, SHRM-SCP, SPHR
Executive Coach and Professional Speaker
Author, *Rethinking Human Resources* and *Humans@Work*

🌐 NallyGroup.com
💼 LinkedIn.com/in/JeffNally

Chapter One

MARIA BAKER

"Welcome Millennials! There's Room for Us All at the Top"

We all want to win! Many of us are striving to get to the top, but we find ourselves fighting with others to get there. Often, we are fighting among generations ... specifically with Generation Y, also known as Millennials. As I sit down to write this book chapter, it's 2019 and Millennials make up the largest portion of our workforce. In order to be successful in the workplace, we must learn to adapt to their needs. We need to welcome the Millennials and find room for them at the top.

"I WANT WHAT YOU WANT AND A LITTLE MORE"

Imagine yourself preparing a job offer for a Millennial candidate. In the prior emails she sent to you, the candidate had a few questions:

- What is your organization's stance on diversity and inclusion?
- Does your organization offer telecommuting or flexible work arrangements?
- What type of career development programs does your company provide?
- What is the starting pay?

Perhaps you, too, have heard these questions before. These are not new, but are surely more common questions during the hiring process now that we're all hiring savvy, modern Millennials. The key is not just anticipating them, but having organizational cultures, processes, policies and attitudes that provide appealing answers to this vital segment of the workforce. Let's explore these top four questions, and their implications and opportunities for your organization ...

⑦ MILLENNIAL QUESTION
"What is your organization's stance on diversity and inclusion?"

This question is multi-layered. It isn't just about underrepresented ages, gender and race. Millennials want to see a diverse mix of experiences, ideas and opinions ... a more collaborative environment. They want to work in an environment that is inclusive of people like them. A diverse organization does a better job attracting a talented workforce. We have to be careful not to overlook all the kinds of diversity that count, because often we are attracted to people in interviews who remind us of ourselves (in background, thought, education and more). We perpetuate sameness. Organizations have to abandon that tendency and remember the goal. Millennials want to make sure that the organization will be inclusive of their thoughts and ideas. And, really, who *wouldn't* want that?

⑦ MILLENNIAL QUESTION
"Does your organization offer telecommuting or flexible work arrangements?"

Millennials want flex time. They want the ability to select when they start and finish their work day. They want the flexibility to choose to work from home, or from an alternative work location.

Consider this case in point: Nicholas Bloom is a Stanford professor who conducted an experiment with a Chinese company called Ctrip. Ctrip is located in Shanghai, which is known to have very expensive property rates. Ctrip wanted to grow without increasing their office space, so they selected a large number of employees to work from home, and the remaining worked in the office. This experiment lasted for two years and Bloom was able to find out that productivity amongst the telecommuters was equivalent to a full day's work in the office headquarters. Ctrip showed a 13% improvement in performance, resignations dropped by 50%, and they made $2,000 more profit per employee. This is phenomenal and supports the great debate of working from home.[1]

See page 10 for practical tips on how to implement flexible work arrangements at your organization!

⑦ MILLENNIAL QUESTION
"What types of career development programs does your company provide?"

This generation is more driven, very ambitious and loves to learn. Most Millennial men and women want training that can help them develop their leadership and management skills so they can quickly move to the top. Millennials are often looked at as the generation that's in a hurry. Millennials were born during the birth of the internet, where everything is fast, accessible and rich with information. It only makes sense for Millennials to want to move quickly, and development will surely get them there. So what can you do to develop your Millennials? Create position leveling that will allow your Millennials to move within the position. Position leveling is when you systematically define the skills, knowledge and abilities that are necessary to establish the duties and

---

1   Bloom, Nicholas, "Go Ahead, Tell Your Boss You Are Working From Home," TedX Stanford, 2017, https://www.youtube.com/watch?v=oiUyyZPIHyY.

5 TIPS FOR IMPLEMENTING FLEXIBLE WORK ARRANGEMENTS AT YOUR COMPANY

1. **Identify the problem.** You first need to ask yourself if you're trying to resolve a problem. Do you need to cut down on real estate costs? Has your organization run out of space? Or do you just want to offer options to help employees with work/life balance, while ensuring your organization remains competitive in the workforce? Whatever your impetus, decide if there is a problem that should be addressed so that you will select the appropriate flexible work arrangement(s) to achieve your goals.

2. **Garner buy-in.** You need to make sure your management team is on board. Will they support your recommendation for flexible work arrangements? One of the most common failures of flexible work arrangements is a lack of management support and commitment. They may think it's too much to manage or that the flexible work arrangement that you are recommending is not going to work in their department or business unit. If that's the case, you may need to provide training to your managers, showing them how to manage the program and helping them see and embrace the benefits of flexible work arrangements to the organization and to their team.

responsibilities of the job. This is positive, as employees will immediately see that you are offering them opportunities for advancement. A great example of this is a Customer Service Representative I, Customer Service Representative II and a Customer Service Representative III.

I also recommend you offer a collection of ongoing learning options like:

3. **Review interrelated policies.** Please understand that as you implement flexible work arrangements, other HR functions could be impacted and you may need to update those policies. For example, you may have to look at updating your performance management practices to include performance goals from teleworkers. Or maybe your telework allows for part-time work in which you should look at updating your compensation and benefits program to allow benefits for part-time workers.

4. **Test, tweak and customize.** Flexible work arrangements are not one-size-fits-all, so you should select the programs that will fit your organization. Before you start a program, try a pilot to test out your assumptions and to make sure the program is exactly what you want. Look for success that will benefit both you and the employees.

5. **Monitor, measure and expand.** Always make sure you monitor success. One of the major mishaps I've seen organizations make when planning for flexible work arrangements is a failure to adequately monitor the success of the program. Companies that fail with flexible work arrangements often wonder why, and subsequently can't explain the failure. The five areas you should monitor after you set up your flexible work arrangements are: costs savings, productivity increase, improved recruiting efforts, lower turnover and improved work/life balance.

- Bringing in guest speakers

- Employee attendance at professional conferences and workshops

- Hosting monthly lunch-and-learn sessions where you allow the employees to get involved in picking up and testing out new skills, knowledge, attitudes and behaviors.

When you promote continuous learning, employees tend to recognize that you're not trying to shelter them, but instead are supporting them to become the best they can be, at your organization and beyond.

⊘ MILLENNIAL QUESTION
"What is the starting pay?"

The talk of the town is that Millennials want money, and then some more money. Without a doubt, Millennials want to make sure they work in a diverse and inclusive environment. They want flexibility and career development too. But these cultural perks don't offset the need to pay employees what they are worth, and Millennials expect you to be fair, competitive and even generous. Money may not be a Millennial's *top* priority, but you better believe it's on the *top 5* list. Many Millennials seldom change jobs without a pay increase. A lot of that has to do with competitors that are already on the cutting edge of technology and are ready to offer Millennials what they want.

UNDERSTANDING WHAT MOTIVATES THE MODERN WORKFORCE

Should organizations just ask Millennials what motivates them? Yes!

So as we look at what Millennials really want, it becomes clear that the questions being asked by job candidates and new hires lead to *motivational answers*. Should organizations just ask Millennials what motivates them? Yes! Millennials are asking these questions in interviews because they know what is needed for them to be motivated. Think about it ... what happens when employees are motivated? They feel

DIFFERENT TYPES OF FLEXIBLE WORK ARRANGEMENTS

- **Telecommuting** (sometimes called remote or virtual work) = Performing a job remotely part of the time and/or when the employee comes to work semi-regularly and can perform the work outside of the traditional office environment.

- **Job sharing** = This is similar to part-time work, where usually two or more part-time workers share a full-time job.

- **Compressed work week** = Where you want the employee to still get their 40 hours in each week, but you are flexible on when and where those hours are completed. For example, you could allow an employee to work four 10-hour days rather than five 8-hour days.

- **Flexible hours** = You allow the employee to choose their own work hours (within reason).

- **Alternate work locations** = A culture in which you allow employees to work at different work locations. Maybe your division has more than one work site that is accessible to everyone.

- **Flexible lunch time** = Where you allow employees to take their lunch break at a time that is beneficial to them.

- **Shift swap** = This allows employees to trade shifts with one another.

satisfied and they work smarter and harder, which ultimately provides the company a positive return on investment. How familiar are you with Herzberg's Two-Factor Theory? This theory says an employee's job satisfaction is influenced by two separate factors. Let's take a look!

Job satisfaction (Motivator factors) = Factors that motivate employees to excellent performance. They are often looked at as satisfying factors, or factors that employees find to be rewarding, in a variety of ways.

Job dissatisfaction (Hygiene factors) = Job factors that are crucial to motivation and work. They typically do not lead to long-term positive satisfaction, but could lead to dissatisfaction if not paired with motivators.

HERZBERG'S TWO-FACTOR THEORY OF MOTIVATION

Job Dissatisfaction	Job Satisfaction
Influenced by Hygiene Factors	**Influenced by Motivator Factors**
• Job security	• Promotion
• Salary	• Status
• Work conditions	• Growth
• Policies	• Recognition
• Supervision	• Responsibility

Here's how I interpret and use the principles first introduced by Herzberg in 1964.

The two-factor theory implies that hygiene factors do not increase satisfaction, but can lead to dissatisfaction if approached or executed poorly. Giving an employee a raise, for example, will provide a short-term motivation, but you should follow up with reward, recognition and career development opportunities, such as:

• Years of service rewards

• Employee appreciation day

- Annual or quarterly bonus

- Social media shout-out

- Extra paid time off

- Effective mentoring programs

- Continuing education opportunities

- Professional organization participation (professional affiliation)

- And more.

WE NEED YOU ON OUR TEAM

Imagine your workplace filled with micromanagement, limited communication, strict boundaries, outdated systems, and no representation of a diverse workforce. Do you think this is the red carpet for an inclusive environment for Millennials? Not at all! Let's dispel the stereotypes and judgments about Millennial professionals, and join forces with them for mutual success.

——————

Imagine your workplace filled with micromanagement, limited communication, strict boundaries, outdated systems, and no representation of a diverse workforce. Do you think this is the red carpet for an inclusive environment for Millennials? Not at all!

——————

A newer generation means new experiences and a new way of thinking. Millennials continue to prove this by bringing fresh ideas and innovative thinking to their companies. They have untapped areas of expertise, comfort and skill that can lead to organizational success, while carrying less career baggage than prior generations. When employees have less career baggage, they tend to be more flexible. It's very challenging when you have employees who are set in their ways and have a now-irrelevant history of expectations from their previous employers. You will be able to train Millennial workers into the perfect employees and leaders for your organization. Millennials are often looked at as out-of-the-box thinkers — just the type of talent needed to deliver a better customer experience, and for your company to gain and keep a competitive edge over your competitors.

Millennials are the most educated and tech-savvy generation to enter the workforce. They are always looking to advance their knowledge, skill and abilities, and are typically fearless about change. Because the internet was born during their time, they eat, drink and sleep technology. They can discover, operate and propose the use of the most advanced systems that are made. In addition, they can give you the upper hand needed to promote your company brand on social media platforms.

You have probably heard of the old phrase "teamwork makes the dream work". Well that phrase is much stronger today than it was 20 years ago. Today, our teams should include a diverse blending of generations to bring about the diverse solutions for success. We *need* Millennials on our team. When we all have like minds to reach a common organizational goal, despite the stereotypical things that make us different, we are coming together to make the dream work ... the dream of organizational success.

———————

When we all have like minds to reach a common organizational goal, despite the stereotypical things that make us different, we are coming together to make the dream work ... the dream of organizational success.

———————

GENERATIONAL CHANGE: SEEING THE NEW EMPLOYEE IN A NEW LIGHT

Imagine you have walked through a time machine and you are at work. You realize you're in another era. People look somewhat the same — their hair and clothes look different, but they are real people ... people you might even recognize. As you start your day at work, you immediately realize so much has changed in such a short period of time. You realize a cultural shift has taken place and you wonder how you got left behind.

That's exactly what happens when we go through generational changes. We wake up and it feels like so much has changed. What has changed is that new groups of professionals are joining our ranks, and we don't recognize the fresh ideas and attitudes they bring with them. Our Millennials are changing expectations and creating a cultural shift to provide a new definition of a good employee. No longer should we look at the number of hours that employees work in a day, but rather look at the quality of what is produced. It's not about the amount of work they get done, but how they go about doing it and the innovative ideas they provide. It's about *results*. And frankly, it always should have been.

Have you thought about the generational differences in your place of work, and how it impacts individuals and teams? Think about how the Traditionalists and Baby Boomers communicate(d) versus how our Millennials communicate today. Many of our Traditionalists don't know how to maneuver through the apps on a smart phone, let alone tweet a story to a group of eager followers. Maybe organizations need to look at Millennials as "the new employee" and put more effort into making sure they — the organizations — do the adapting to better serve them.

Try holding lunch-and-learn sessions that are facilitated by Millennials who can teach fellow employees how to use different social media platforms for business purposes, like tweeting the success of a recent business

THE GENERATIONS, AT A GLANCE

Let's talk about the differences among the generations of workers in today's diverse organizations. You will notice that, individually, these differences are not surprising. But when put into perspective, you may find yourself nodding in agreement, and having "ah ha" epiphanies about how to better understand, reward, treat and collaborate with colleagues across the generations.

Traditionalists (born in or before 1945), also known as The Forgotten Generation, are hard workers, loyal, respect authority, follow the rules and may feel entitled based on seniority.

The Baby Boomers (born between 1946 and 1964) are workaholics, driven, team players, quality is important to them and they may feel entitled based on experience.

Generation Xers (born between 1965 and 1980) are self-sufficient, want equality, tend to be skeptical, want order and leadership, may feel entitled based on merit.

Millennials (born between 1981 and 1997) are multitaskers, they are determined, entrepreneurial, effective workers but will leave work on time and may feel entitled based on their contribution.

project. This is a great way to bring the generations together in the workplace, while embracing the differences that make us unique. I'm a Gen Xer and I am someone who used to prefer to tell someone "thank you" by sending a personal handwritten note. When I shared this with my Millennial peers in the human resources field, a few of them smiled and said they preferred sending a quick email with lots of emoticons.

I eventually changed and got with the new age quickly because I now see that many people want to move fast. Even when you are thanking them, they are already on to the next thing, so I try to keep it short, sweet and sent via email. ☺ But the lessons go both ways; many people, regardless of generation, really appreciate a handwritten thank-you note, so consider doing both to set yourself apart. Send a quick acknowledgment via email today, then drop a personal note into the mail tomorrow.

WE ALL WIN: LEVERAGING MILLENNIAL STEREOTYPES TO PRODUCE A WIN-WIN SITUATION

Let's face it, Millennials often get a bad rap for many of their work characteristics. Society often frowns upon things that they're not used to in the workplace, even if those things are smart, full of potential or a long time coming. If we stop, ask ourselves why Millennials do some of the things they do and before answering ... *think like a Millennial* ... I bet we come up with some pretty good answers. And those answers just might help us turn those negatives into positives. Let's consider accusations about entitlement, technology distractions, job hopping and the demand for more flexible work arrangements.

Entitlement

We know Millennials want to get to the top ... many people do, regardless of when they were born. But Millennials are getting a bad rap, accused of wanting to get to the top quickly and not wanting to work for it. This is looked at as negative ... but why? Let's think like a Millennial and provide answers! Society is used to a traditional work hierarchy, where power flows vertically, where a chain of command exists and where many workplace accomplishments are rewarded with promotions. Baby Boomers want Millennials to pay their dues, just like they did. Boomers want Millennials to work hard, prove themselves and wait for a promotion. So let's all win! Millennials should not have to wait for success. If they have succeeded faster than traditionalists, then let the celebration begin. Millennials must show that they have paid their dues. If a Millennial is ready to respond to a major assignment at work — an assignment that could possibly lead to a future promotion — they should ask their senior colleague to review their work and ask for their feedback. Boomers love to provide feedback, especially when they are asked by Millennials. Getting them involved will make them feel like they are a part of the Millennials' success.

And how about demonstrating greater work ethic? Millennials should go above and beyond the call of duty when finishing an assignment. They should try showing up for work early and staying late when they can. This is much more inclusive and should help squash the negative stereotype that Millennials feel entitled. Little tweaks to how we flex our styles can send strong messages to our colleagues, whether they're younger or older than us.

We live in different times from when many of us started our careers, so don't you think hard work is going to look different? Of course it will. Just because things are moving faster, does not mean that Millennials don't want to work hard. With all the technology that we have right now, we need to focus on productivity and results, rather than face-to-face meeting or outdated status reports. We now have advanced technology that will handle many of the tasks that once occupied much of the day. So instead of worrying about something that you think a Millennial is acting entitled about, maybe focus on how productivity might improve, thanks to their fresh, efficient and focused approaches.

Technology Distractions – "Not at My Table!"

Millennials are also known as digital natives ... those raised in a digitally saturated era. Many earlier generations look at them as lacking focus because they are always on their digital devices, lurking on social media or checking their smartphones. It is the Millennial's responsibility to show his or her manager what helps them at work. Technology does not have to be a distraction. If using technology to view social media helps employees perform their jobs, then Millennials should incorporate social technology into the workplace. Years ago, I used to require those attending my training sessions to leave their cell phones at their desk. I did not want a phone call or an attempt to text to distract them from learning. Furthermore, I didn't want anything to distract me from teaching. As time went on, technology advanced and society became more dependent upon cell phones, and I realized that I had to adjust. While cell phones were a distraction in my training sessions, I also knew that many of the attendees needed to have them for business reasons. Maybe they were waiting on an important call. Maybe they were tweeting about how amazing my training session was!

I realized there were ways to control this and still allow the employees to have their phones on hand. When I started allowing attendees to bring their phones, I told them up front that I wanted all phones on silent or vibrate mode, so we could reduce distractions. I then took away the one big break and gave two smaller breaks to allow them time to check email and return a quick call. This seemed to work well. Again ... we had a win-win situation.

But not all GenXers, Baby Boomers or Traditionalists are yet embracing the value of the average Millennial's comfort and reliance upon technology. So, what's a Millennial to do? At the next staff meeting, Millennials should show their managers an article on something hot in their industry that was recently posted on Instagram or Twitter, especially if it's news about a competitor. We must remember that the internet is the core of constantly changing information and building lasting contacts. The world is changing daily and it's important to keep updated on business trends to help stay on top of the competition. Eventually the manager will see how technology and social media does have a seat at the table.

Job Hopping

How long should one stay at a job? And if you're happy, why leave ... ever? Millennials are getting a bad rap because they are known to leave companies after a year or two. So, let's think like a Millennial! Why would a Millennial want to leave a company after a year? It's possible they are not engaged. Many organizations are missing the mark on this one. It may come across that Millennials want more, when actually they just want a job that makes them feel like it's worth their effort. I hired a Millennial who I'll call Jack. A year after Jack was hired, he approached his manager about more job responsibilities and an increase in pay. His manager couldn't make any promises, but assured Jack that she would talk to HR to see what she could do, because, after all, Jack was out-producing all his peers, even those who had more experience than him.

HR informed Jack's manager that there was a position one step higher than Jack's position and he could be promoted into it, as long as he was the most qualified candidate. Well, Jack ended up being promoted and received a 15% pay increase. About eight months later, Jack tendered his resignation and went to work for another company as a manager, where he was responsible for a small team and made 33% more than he did with us. So what happened here? Jack went to his manager for a promotion and more money and he got it. Why did he leave eight months later? Was that not enough? I talked to Jack and I asked him those questions. And here's what he told me: He left because the promotion that he received did not *fulfill* him. He did get an increase in his work load, but it was the same work he was already doing … just more of it. And extra pay for extra work doesn't make a position extra rewarding. Jack also said that he was promoted into the top position in that role and there wasn't any other place to go. Jack said that he wanted challenging work that was different from what he was already doing, something that would lead to management.

So, is leaving something *good* because you found something *better* truly bad? Of course not. Maybe your Millennials, too, are leaving because they've found a better fit for their career aspirations. Some smaller companies struggle in this area because they are less likely to be able to move their Millennials up the career ladder as fast as larger companies. Smaller companies must make sure they provide the culture Millennials want and offer as many perks as they can to increase employee retention.

Why does quitting a job feel like it's wrong? Maybe because many decisions are made based on what society expects, rather than what you really need. When you make your decision to leave a job, you are in control and are able to choose your next step. This doesn't mean you don't have the skills, knowledge or ability to do the job. Maybe the door opened for you to make a career decision and it was simply time to move. Millennials get that, and so should we.

Flexible Work Schedules

As I said earlier, Millennials want flexible work arrangements. Millennials realize that it's no longer necessary to be physically in the office to complete your work. Regardless where you are, technology will allow you to log into your computer and work, communicate and stay informed. Other generations frown on this because they feel Millennials will be less productive and sloppy with their work. But, frankly, this will only happen if you don't set goals, motivate and oversee the process (and hire trustworthy, motivated employees in the first place). So, what are some types of flexible work arrangements? Telecommuting, working part time, flexible work hours and freelancing (see the sidebar on page 13 for more details). What are some of the benefits for providing a flexible work arrangement to your employees? Oh, so many. Here are the top five.

An increase in job satisfaction. For some, working in an office can be very confining. My friend Lisa, who is a Millennial, said a fluffy couch sounds so much better. She also said that she is much more creative and motivated when working from home. She accomplishes more work faster, and produces a higher quality product.

Time saved. In many large metropolitan areas, traffic can be horrendous and can take many travelers an hour or even two hours to get to work (round trip). It's my experience that employees who are "gifted" those hours back each day, show up to their virtual office more energized and engaged, and that some even work an extra hour or two (from home, comfortably and focused) as they reallocate the time they used to spend in the car or on the train.

Work/life balance. Job satisfaction and productivity is always high when work arrangements are flexible. Calling out because someone is sick is, conversely, usually low. Allowing employees to manage their schedule and environment allows them to create a better work/life balance. The fact that some companies are able to provide the balance that Millennials seek shows that the wellbeing of employees is important to management, and Millennials want to give their company their best in return.

Lower turnover. There is a high cost when you lose employees. And the losses aren't just monetary. When turnover is high, employee moral decreases, you lose productivity, you have increased customer errors, etc. Offering flexible work arrangements lowers your turnover and, hence, saves you money in many ways.

Attracting the cream of the crop. If you don't offer flexible work arrangements, then your competitor will. We are living in a society where technology allows organizations to offer a variety of flexible options. Millennials want flexibility. When you can give them what they want, you will often attract the best in the business.

If you don't offer flexible work arrangements, then your competitor will.

"IF I STAY ... MENTOR ME AND HELP ME TO THE TOP"

With stereotypes dispelled and objections to the demands of Millennials addressed by the recommendations of this book chapter, there's just one thing left to tackle: Giving Millennials the experienced advisors they need so they can rise. Millennials may need mentors to help them along the way, and mentors are truly deserved by this vital segment of the workforce. I'm not talking about just any garden-variety mentor relationship, either. I believe a Millennial professional needs a mentor where both parties have a mutual relationship and a vested interest in each other — where the mentor can put aside preconceived notions that he or she may have, and help guide and focus the mentee to grow as a leader. To get this type of mentorship for your employees, you might have to work with your human resources department to revamp what you already have in place. If you have a traditional mentorship program, it's probably set up by human resources and involves younger employees being matched with those in higher levels of management. The process may include the manager checking in with them from time to time and providing an evaluation at the end of a predetermined mentoring timeframe. Not only is that process outdated, but Millennials are not having it.

Millennials want more effective and faster mentor programs. They need someone who has a vested interest in their future and someone who won't just tell them "here's what I did when I was in your role," but challenge them to think outside the box. Millennials need and deserve frequent communication and feedback. They should be allowed to make mistakes, so they can learn how to bounce back up and try again. If you have the opportunity to mentor a Millennial, be honest 100% of the time, show respect and lead by example.

In the end, Millennials truly want careers that are fulfilling, and good mentors can help a great deal. Be sure to check out Chapter 5 of this book for Michael Rider's insights on mentoring. He talks about mentoring as a business catalyst and how mentoring is the super highway to engagement. I especially like how he refers to mentoring as magic because I, too, believe mentoring is like magic ... the power of influence.

Let's Reverse It!

As mentors and mentees are paired, make sure you find out what each person would like to know more about. Just as Millennials can have an experienced and trusted advisor, so can other generations. Have you heard of reverse mentoring? The concept of reverse mentoring is when older executives are paired with younger employees who teach them about new technology and social media. Reverse mentoring recognizes that there are skills gaps on both sides and each party can use their skill to help each other. Having a mentor and a mentee who both share in the role of being the mentor is a recipe for success. It allows a Millennial to get the advisement they need, and also allows the executive to learn more about things like social media and technology. Reverse mentorship will allow the older generations to add to their skillsets and feel more valued and engaged along the way. Millennials will feel empowered and are less likely leave your organization in search of a more attractive environment.

If you haven't seen the movie *The Intern*, let me suggest you do. It's about a 70-year-old widower, Ben, who is bored with retired life and applies for a "senior" intern position at an online fashion retailer. The word "senior" does not mean a 12th grader in high school; it means a senior citizen. Ben gets hired as the senior intern and has no clue about social media and new age technology, much less modern work etiquette or dress codes. His co-workers are always helping him out with email, setting up social media accounts, upgrading his cell phone, etc. Conversely, Ben helps his younger colleagues with dating, how to dress for success, making smart decisions about life, how to deal with marriage complications, and more. While this isn't a formal "mentor program," per se, the movie illustrates what is clearly a great example of reverse mentoring. What a great way to help bridge the gap between generations and get away from the "us versus them" argument.

READY OR NOT, HERE THEY COME!

Every organization must find a way to incorporate and adapt to Millennials — to embrace the inspiration and fresh talent they bring. The prior years of traditional upward power are gone. Today, we need teamwork, not hierarchies.

Every organization must find a way to incorporate and adapt to Millennials — to embrace the inspiration and fresh talent they bring. The prior years of traditional upward power are gone. Today, we need teamwork, not hierarchies. As organizations welcome Millennials to every leadership level — including the C-suite — they do so knowing that healthy partnership among generations is paramount to success. It's without a doubt that all CEOs will eventually be Millennials, but will they be ready? We know they are highly engaged, eager to learn and have lots of ambition. We also know that Millennials are digital natives, which will position them for technological success. *But will they be ready?* It's up to us.

Let's recognize what the future holds. Let's share our seats. Let's slide over and let them sit next to us, while we advise them, guide them and provide constant communication to them. When they fall, we'll be there to encourage them to get up and keep pressing forward. That's what they want and what they deserve. And if we don't give it to them, eagerly and with open minds, *we'll fail* and *they'll leave* to succeed somewhere else. It's time to see Millennials as an investment in the future of our businesses and our careers, and to start doing all we must to protect that precious investment.

ABOUT THE AUTHOR

Maria Baker
MS HRM, CCC

Maria Baker is the founder and CEO of HR Smart, LLC, a human resources consulting company that provides HR management services to small and mid-sized organizations that lack dedicated full-time HR leadership. Maria has more than 20 years in human resources, and has worked for companies within various industries, like manufacturing, healthcare, telecommunications, corrections, and education. She thrives on helping companies stay compliant in a forever-changing environment. Her recent professional focus encompasses millennials in the workplace and organizations that are not adapting to the changes necessary to be successful with a millennial-dominated workforce.

Maria is a member of the Millennial Chamber of Commerce, a member of the Georgia Diversity Council and a member of the Society of Human Resources Management (SHRM). She also volunteers as a Career Coach for Single Mothers Matter, an organization that helps single mothers create self-sufficiency by providing support services, skills training and guidance in pursuing life's purpose. Maria has facilitated career seminars with the Georgia Department of Labor and has been the guest speaker at various career seminars hosted by Goodwill of North Georgia.

Maria holds a Master's degree in human resources management, a Bachelor's degree in interdisciplinary studies and an Associate's degree in business management. She is a Certified Career Coach who helps define, redefine and achieve professional objectives. Maria lives in

Conyers, Georgia, with her husband of 24 years and their two daughters. She enjoys crafting and spending time with her family.

Learn more and contact Maria:

- ✉ Maria.Baker@HRsmartLLC.org
- 🔗 LinkedIn.com/in/MariaBaker-MSHRM
- 🌐 HRsmartLLC.org

Chapter Two - Part One

MICHELE FANTT HARRIS

"Coaching in the Workplace"

Everyone is familiar with the sports coach who develops young athletes into the winning team. Coaching in the workplace is similar but there are differences as well. Both the workplace coach and the sports coach want to develop each team member to be a better performer. Sports coaches are often demanding and forceful in their approach while, in the workplace, coaching is a collaborative effort. In the business environment, coaches want to identify a goal, set a target for performance and develop a plan of action to improve the employee's performance.

In sports coaching, the coaches are usually experts in the field and were previous athletes themselves. In the workplace, however, a great coach might not share the same functional expertise as the employee, who is responsible for his or her own development, while the coach provides resources and support. To be a good workplace coach, you don't need to have knowledge or work experience in the employee's field of endeavor; in fact, great leaders and great coaches often provide guidance to employees whose education, experience or functional expertise exceeds or differs from their own. And strong workplace coaches don't always come from within the same organizations. Many organizations use independent coaches or coaching firms to train employees and managers how to coach. Coaching can be difficult for the employees' direct managers, as they are used to directing work rather than achieving results through coaching and development. Coaches act as facilitators to help employees achieve their desired performance by asking probing and difficult questions that challenge the employee to reflect on their goals, as well as plan for development and growth. Direct managers use the "tell" approach to help and improve employee performance, but a good coach uses the "ask" approach that helps the employee to remove barriers to enable them to act on their existing knowledge and skills.

Coaches act as facilitators to help employees achieve their desired performance by asking probing and difficult questions that challenge the employee to reflect on their goals, as well as plan for development and growth.

COACHING IS NOT …

For leaders who are new to coaching in the workplace, it can be easier to first understand what coaching is *not*, before embarking on the vital work of understanding and actualizing what coaching *is*.

Coaching is not a disciplinary action. Coaching should not occur when there are performance deficiencies. Employees who are not performing to satisfactory standards should be placed on a performance improvement plan (PIP) or performance action plan. These plans are used when the employee has the necessary skills to perform the job and there is a commitment on the manager's part to help the employee succeed.

Coaching is not psychotherapy. Coaching does not seek to treat psychological problems, such as depression or anxiety. Coaching is focused on the present and future or forward thinking, while psychotherapy is focused on the past and present or healing an employee's troubled or fragile mental state. Employees who have serious problems — such as drug and alcohol abuse or mental health issues — should be directed to a professional who can provide the professional and individualized healthcare that they need.

Coaching is not counseling. At times during a coaching session, a personal issue will be addressed that impacts an employee's professional life. The coach might help the employee realize the impact of the personal problem and how it is affecting the employee's work performance. The coach will work with the employee to plan actions to keep work performance high while addressing their personal issues on their own. It is not the coach's place to provide counseling on the personal issues themselves, but to acknowledge the interconnectedness between our work lives and our personal lives, and guide the employee as he or she works to keep things in balance.

Coaching is not mentoring. Mentors are usually experts or guides who help employees who need advice or direction. Mentors provide guidance on problem-solving issues or help employees navigate issues. Mentors are often solution-focused. Employees seek advice from their mentor and usually follow through on the advice given because the mentor has direct experience and knowledge of the employee's role and situation in the company. But coaches fill a somewhat different role, questioning their clients or employees to help them resolve the issues on their own. Coaches typically believe that you are the expert on your life and your career, and that it's their job to help you uncover the answers that already lie within your mindset.

THE BENEFITS OF COACHING

Coaching in business and leadership settings is an important tool for developing employees across a wide range of needs. According to a 2009 report by the International Coaching Federation, 80% of people who receive workplace coaching report increased self-confidence, and more than 70% benefit from improved work performance, workplace relationships and more effective communication skills. A staggering 86% of companies report that they recuperated their investment on coaching.[1]

The benefits of coaching in organizations are many. Coaching:

- Empowers employees to establish and take action toward achieving their goals

- Increases employee engagement

- Helps employees become more self-reliant

- Helps organizations and managers to identify and develop high-potential employees

- Helps employees gain more job and life satisfaction

- Demonstrates the company's commitment to talent development.

CAN ANYONE BE A GOOD COACH?

Coaches come from a wide variety of disciplines and backgrounds, including business consulting, human resources, organizational development and training, as well as sports and education arenas. I recommend that you consider working with a coach who is certified through the International Coach Federation (ICF), International Association of Coaching (IAC) or Worldwide Association of Business Coaches (WABC), or who has completed a certified training programing, though

---

1   International Coach Federation, "Coaching Overview," 2009.

I have met some very good coaches who are not certified. I suggest you have an exploratory meeting with a potential coach. Most coaches will provide a complimentary coaching session to see if rapport is easily established and whether a good working relationship exists.

There is not a one-size-fits-all approach to coaching, but most successful coaches have a few important things in common. They listen well. They hold employees accountable. They are inquisitive and encouraging. They deliver clear, effective feedback. And they exhibit strong emotional intelligence and earn the trust that this placed in them. To be effective, coaches must be present and attuned to the client or employee's current state. Being present allows coaches to provide an atmosphere of trust, safety and confidentiality.

Anyone can be taught coaching skills, but most professional coaches are certified through the International Coach Federation or other certified coaching program. Certification through ICF demonstrates that the coach has completed a coaching training program and has completed many hours of practical coaching. While I had a natural love and affinity for coaching employees before I underwent my coaching certification training, what I learned through the process has enabled me to use the right questions and techniques to help employees move their careers forward. I no longer suggest the career path they take; I help them map out their own path according to their desires, interests and career aspirations.

THE GROW MODEL

Coaches help employees make better decisions, solve problems, learn new skills and develop in their careers. A simple coaching practice for helping employees is the GROW Model of Coaching.

The GROW model was developed 30 years ago by the late Sir John Whitmore and was published in his book *Coaching for Performance*.[2] GROW is a coaching model that provides a framework for the coaching conversation or meeting. It enables employees to move forward toward positive outcomes and achievements.

GROW
Goal **+** Reality Check **+** Options **+** Will

The acronym GROW stands for Goal + Reality Check + Options + Will. This four-step progression leads the employee from defining the objective (Goal), to examining the current reality (Reality Check), to exploring courses of action (Options) and finally to developing concrete action steps (Will) to moving toward the goal.

I find the GROW Model very easy to follow as a manager or a coach. It is straightforward and puts the employee in control of their own destiny. The employee develops their own steps toward achieving their goal, which helps gain employee commitment in solving problems and achieving work success.

The GROW Model is similar to planning a trip. First, you decide where you are going to travel (the goal) and establish where you currently are (your reality check of the means of transportation, your financial state, etc.). You then explore various routes and ways (the options) to your destination. In the final step, you establish the will, ensure that you are committed to making the journey and are prepared for any obstacles you could meet on the way.

---

2   Whitmore, Sir John, *Coaching for Performance: The Principles and Practice of Coaching and Leadership*, Nicholas Brealey Publishing Company, 2017, 5th edition.

I strongly encourage HR professionals who are new to coaching to use the GROW Model, as it is easy and simple for the coach and the employee to understand and follow. To structure a coaching session using the GROW Model, follow the following steps:

1. Establish the Goal

In *Alice in Wonderland* by Lewis Carroll, Alice said in her conversation with the Cheshire cat:

Alice: Would you tell me, please which way I ought to go from here?

Cat: That depends a good deal on where you want to get to.

Alice: I don't much care where.

Cat: Then it does not matter which way.

As the Cheshire cat implied, if you don't know where you are going, any road will do. When employees identify what they want to achieve, it changes their mindset to action to solve the dilemma.

As the Cheshire cat implied, if you don't know where you are going, any road will do. When employees identify what they want to achieve, it changes their mindset to action to solve the dilemma.

As a coach, you should work with employees to identify what behavior they want to change and then structure this change as a goal to be achieved. When employees identify what they want to achieve, they find themselves on a path to accomplishing the goal by focusing on the solution rather than on the problem.

The goal should ideally be developed as a SMART goal – one that is *Specific* (states exactly what is to be achieved), *Measurable* (establishes clear definitions to help you measure if the goal is reached.), *Action-Oriented* (described using action words and an outline of the steps needed to accomplish the goal.), *Realistic* (reasonable and attainable) and *Time-Bound* (with a definition for the amount of time needed to start and finish goal).

Some **Goal Questions** that a coach might ask include:

- What, specifically, do you want to accomplish?
- Over what time frame?
- Where would you like to be, at that end point, on a scale of 1 to 10 in terms of job satisfaction or accomplishment?
- How can you say your goal in just a few words?
- How will you know when you have achieved your goal? What will success look like? Can you measure it?
- In an ideal world, what do you *really* want?

2. Examine the Current Reality

At this step, the coach asks the employee for a reality check to determine an objective starting point for the desired change. The coach is trying to get the employee to ascertain the concrete facts pertaining to how things stand now. Do not try to solve the problem without first fully understanding where the employee is now.

Some **Reality Questions** that a coach might ask include:

- When was the last time that happened?
- What is happening now (who, what, when and how often)? What is the effect or result of this?

- What have you tried already? What difference did those actions make?

- What events or choices led you to this place?

- Does this goal conflict with any other goals or objectives?

- Which factors are most important in this matter?

3. Explore the Options

Once the employees have explored their current situation or reality, it's time to develop several possible solutions. The coach helps the employees to brainstorm as many options as possible, and then helps the employees to decide on the best alternatives. It is important for the coach to let the employees do most of the talking and to guide them in the right direction for them, without actually making the decision for them.

Possible **Options Questions** that a coach might ask include:

- What else could you do?

- Let's try to create at least five potential solutions.

- If you had unlimited resources and knew you could not fail, what would you try?

- What are the advantages and disadvantages of each option?

- What factors or considerations will you use to weigh the options?

- What if this obstacle was removed? What would you do then?

- What could you do to overcome this obstacle? What are your options?

- Who could help you?

- What other resources could you draw on to tackle this?

- What do you need to stop doing in order to achieve this goal?

- What have you seen others do that might work for you?

I recently coached a recruiter about her options for using her current skills to enhance and develop her career. She enjoys recruiting because she works with a diverse set of clients and enjoys working for search firms, but she wants to do more than be a recruiter. I asked her what does "more" look like. She began to talk about learning the recruiting business — understanding how the company works at every level. We discussed how she could learn the business — shadow the firm's operating officer, solicit a new business client for the firm and work with the client from beginning to the end of the search, represent the company at trade shows, attend recruiting conferences to learn how competing search firms operate, talk to the firm's CEO to see how he started the business, etc. After we developed and discussed at least five options, we discussed what she could do immediately. She decided to talk to the firm's CEO to discuss the business and then to ask the CEO or COO if she could shadow them on special assignments with new clients. She really enjoys the firm where she currently is employed but wants to learn more of the operations side of the recruiting business. If she enjoys the operations side as much as she enjoys the recruiting, she will eventually open her own recruiting firm.

4. ESTABLISH THE WILL

Now that the employees have examined the current reality and explored their options, the employees have a good idea how they can achieve their goal. At this step, the coach helps the employees change the preferred solution into concrete action steps with high buy-in from the employee. This step is called "Will" rather than "Action" to stress that the coach must ensure that the action is one the employee can really commit to. The coach helps the employee establish the will and boost the employee's motivation.

Possible **Will Questions** that a coach might ask include:

- What will you do now, and what will be completed by the time of our next meeting? What else will you do?

- What could stop you moving forward? How will you overcome this?

- How can you keep yourself motivated?

- What option(s) do you want to pursue?

- What step could you take this week that would move you toward your goal?

- You mentioned that you could do _____. What will you commit to doing?

Consider how to use the GROW Model in a way that fits your own style, as well as the needs of your coaches. The stages of the GROW model don't always need to occur in the order I've laid them out in this book chapter. An effective coaching conversation usually starts by exploring Goal and Reality, but then moves about between all four elements in an organic and sometimes circuitous manner. The actual questions asked are often not as important as deciding which stage of the model will be most useful to the employee at any given moment.

For example, imagine you are helping — coaching — a team member, Rick, to achieve his goal using the GROW Model. Rick would like to be promoted to a manager role within the next two years. This is a SMART goal — it is specific, measurable and attainable. There are several manager roles within the company for which he can apply. The goal is relevant because it meets his career aspirations, and because several managers will retire in two years.

You and Rick look at his current reality. He has one year on this job as an underwriter but was a manager at his previous job, so he has some managerial skills. You brainstorm the additional skills that he will need in order to be successful in a manager role: He needs more experience in managing his current team, and he needs to accept the role for team lead on projects to be seen as a leader by his team. He also needs to continue to perform well in his role by taking on more complex assignments, so he will be considered for a managerial promotion when one is available.

You then review his options. To get the managerial experience he needs, Rick could lead a team on a small project. He could volunteer to train new underwriters to the team. He could volunteer to lead other "action learning teams" in the organization.

Finally, you establish the will. Rick agrees with his manager that he will train all new underwriters and will take on more complex underwriting assignments. His manager assigns him to fill in for her when she is out of the office, which will allow his team members to see him in the management role. He continues to perform well and takes on these new assignments, and ultimately the manager agrees to recommend him for the next promotion.

COACHING IS A GIFT

Coaching provides an invaluable space for personal and professional development.

In the end, being coached in the workplace can open doors and help employees achieve their goals. And being a coach is a power and a privilege. Organizations that commit to the value of coaching are organizations that are setting themselves up for higher engagement, better internal relations and lower turnover.

Coaching provides an invaluable space for personal and professional development. Although external behavior may change as a result of coaching, true coaching is supported by changes in the employee's internal thought processes. Effective coaching can increase an employee's self-confidence and makes employees more resilient.

Coaching helps to change an employee's attitude or mindset, which is the one thing with which HR professionals and managers universally struggle. You know the old adage that "you can lead a horse to the water but you can't make it drink." Well, a good coach can get the horse to drink ... can encourage and motivate the employee to change their behavior and their attitude. Coaching delves into the inner mind of your employees — their fears, anxieties, strengths, weaknesses, positive and negative feelings, and aspirations. Coaches and managers are important guides who simply ask questions to the employees and allow the employees to "unearth" what is hindering them to maximizing their full potential in their jobs, their work and in their daily lives.

Chapter Two - Part Two

MICHELE FANTT HARRIS

"Exit Interview vs. Stay Interview"

I dedicate this chapter to Marjorie Lee Silber, who encouraged me to write an article about exit interviews and the value that they hold for an organization. You see, Marjorie had resigned from her manager position in the Servicing Department at a large non-profit organization, and I conducted an exit interview with her. During our exit interview, I discovered that Marjorie really enjoyed working for the organization. She believed in the mission of the organization, liked the people and enjoyed the work, but she did not like her boss.

As I talked to Marjorie, I learned more about her knowledge, skills and abilities, and found her to be a perfect fit for the Membership Manager position in another division at another location of the organization. Marjorie had the management skills that were required for the Membership position; all she needed was to learn the various membership categories and its members. And, as it turned out, she didn't already have another job lined up at another organization. So, I immediately arranged an interview for her with the other division. She was interviewed and was hired the same day! She had resigned her Servicing position on Friday and started in the Membership Manager job the following

Monday. She was able to retain her benefits without a lapse in coverage, and the organization was able to keep a valuable employee. Talk about win-win! Marjorie remained at the organization for another 10 years after receiving the new job.

This unique and powerful experience taught me the value of both exit interviews and stay interviews. I started an exit interview with Marjorie, but when I discovered her valuable skills, I changed the exit interview into a stay interview. Employers conduct exit interviews to get feedback about the job the employee held, the work environment and the company. Exit interviews provide honest feedback about company culture, morale, fringe benefits, management, teams and specific jobs. Most terminating employees will be very free with information about the company and culture. They have nothing to gain or lose, especially if they are leaving for another job or relocating out of the area.

Most terminating employees will be very free with information about the company and culture. They have nothing to gain or lose, especially if they are leaving for another job or relocating out of the area.

FUNDAMENTALS OF A GOOD EXIT INTERVIEW

Exit interviews can provide Human Resources valuable information about recruitment, onboarding and training needs for the organization. The feedback that you receive will help you to identify areas that can help improve employee retention. The information can also help you improve the organization's culture in areas such as management development and succession planning.

Exit interviews should be standard procedure for offboarding and should be voluntary. Mandatory exit interviews rarely give you good information to help the company. If an employee refuses the exit interview, you might ask her if you can follow-up with her in six months. Employees should not be penalized if they fail to participate in the exit interview, and exit interviews are conducted with employees who leave the company voluntarily. Exit interviews should be granted to all departing employees and not just key personnel or long-term employees.

To encourage employees to participate, exit interview discussions should be confidential. I make a point to tell employees how I will use the information that is collected during the exit interview. I provide one report to senior management at the end of the year, which does not list names, dates or specific employee feedback that would identify the terminating employee who gave the information. I explain that the information is used by the company to help improve working conditions, training and career development, and employee engagement.

I do inform departing employees that if they report any criminal behavior, sexual harassment or incidents of discrimination or risk non-compliance issues, then I have a responsibility to take further action. One of the exit interview questions that I ask is, "Are you aware of any compliance or risk management issues that were not appropriately addressed by either your manager or others within the company?" This question allows a departing employee to freely talk about a harassment or bullying incident that may be occurring in the employee's department or within the company. Although asking the question in the exit interview may not change the decision of the employee to leave, it might save other employees from leaving the company if appropriate action is taken.

Exit interviews should be conducted by Human Resources or a neutral manager who is trained in active listening. Some companies outsource exit interviews to an independent third party. I tend to conduct exit interviews with the departing employee before they leave the organization. Other employers may contact the former employee three to six months after they have left the organization. Other employers conduct an exit interview before *and* after the employee leaves, to ascertain whether the employee will later give the same reason for leaving as they stated in their initial exit interview meeting.

Many employees provide departing employees with an exit interview questionnaire or provide an online exit interview using a service like SurveyMonkey. I find it particularly useful to follow up the questionnaire with an interview. Survey answers sometimes surface issues that need to be "unpacked" further. Many powerful insights may be discovered during the exit interview discussion, which the employee would not disclose in the written questionnaire. Other employers prefer casual one-on-one discussions, where the employee talks freely and the interviewer takes notes.

To get valuable information from the exit interview, you need to ask the right questions to gain a deep insight into your employees and the company. Here is a list of exit interview questions. There is no right or wrong answer to these questions.[1]

What to Ask the Employee in an Exit Interview

1. Why are you leaving your job?
2. If your reason for leaving was a new job, what does this job offer to you that your position at this company did not?
3. Describe what you liked best about working with our company.
4. Describe what you liked least about working with our company.

---

[1]   Some of the questions in my list were derived from the article, "Stay Interview vs. Exit Interview," McCloskey Partners, LLC, June 5, 2017. Others are my own.

5. How did you feel about the supervision, training and performance coaching that you received for your current job?

6. Do you have any recommendations for the company for the future?

7. What advice would you give your replacement if you could?

8. How would you describe the culture of our company?

9. What could have been done for you to remain employed here?

10. How do you feel about the feedback and support that you received from your manager?

11. What was your best day on the job like? What was your worst day on the job like?

12. What can the company do to become the employer of choice in our industry?

13. What was the biggest factor that led you to accept your new job?

14. What skills and qualifications do you think we need to look for in your replacement?

15. How has your job description changed during your employment in this job?

16. What was the best part of your job? Why?

17. What was the worst part of your job? Why?

18. How would you improve employee morale?

19. Would you recommend this company to a friend who was looking for a job?

20. Are you aware of any compliance or risk management issues that were not appropriately addressed by either your manager or others within the company?

21. Do you have any other issues or comments that you would like to address?

22. What question are you glad that I did not ask?

FUNDAMENTALS OF A GOOD STAY INTERVIEW

Many human resources professionals prefer stay interviews rather than exit interviews. Stay interviews are two-way conversations between an employee and manager or human resources professional to discover what employees like and don't like about their job and the work environment. Stay interviews allow you to make changes before employees leave and may result in reduced employee turnover.

Stay interviews are a *proactive* approach to soliciting feedback about what motivates and engages employees. Stay interviews gives the company valuable information about employee engagement and what may cause an employee to leave the organization. Exit interviews, on the other hand, are a *reactive* approach to determine why an employee is leaving the company. At the time of the exit interview, the employee has already made the decision to leave the company. Exit interview situations like the one involving Marjorie Walker are rare, where the company was able to salvage the employment relationship.

Some employees don't give honest feedback in an exit interview situation because they don't believe that their feedback will change things in the department or at the company. Stay interviews, however, tend to get more valuable insight about employee concerns. In a stay interview, the employee feels valued and feels the company cares about their opinions. They are likely to believe the company will make the necessary changes to keep the employee engaged. Stay interviews allow managers and employees to work collaboratively toward creating a better work environment and positive company culture.

Internal stay interviews should be conducted by an employee's manager on a regular basis and can be conducted with an employee appraisal or an employee development meeting. The key is to get in front of potential problems and correct employee dissatisfaction issues before they evolve.

Human Resources may conduct random stay interviews with employees after an employee opinion survey. The stay interview gives the HR professional more in-depth information than what was provided in the opinion/satisfaction survey.

Stay interviews are most effective when the company's leadership is committed to making positive changes based on employees' feedback. If changes result due to the stay interviews, leadership needs to acknowledge the change was based on employee feedback. This acknowledgement will encourage greater participation and honest feedback in future stay interviews. Failure to follow through on employer commitments will jeopardize leadership's credibility and result in the loss of employee trust.

Stay interviews may be conducted externally by a third-party consultant to understand the employee's intent to stay or leave the organization and why. External stay interviews are used to assess if certain groups of employees may be at a higher risk of turnover, and/or to identify high-potential employees for the company. These external stay interviews are usually high-quality, one-on-one interviews to drive high retention and engagement. Stay interviews are an integral part of an effective retention strategy.

Many managers are reluctant to conduct stay interviews for fear that employees will ask for a salary raise that is not in the budget. This fear is largely unfounded. Employees are usually very grateful to be asked their opinions about the company and what makes them want to stay or leave. Engaging the employee in an open dialogue is viewed favorably and that you value their feedback.

Asking the right questions in a stay interview is very important. Below are some questions that can be asked to get a sense of what makes your employees successful at work.[2]

What to Ask the Employee in a Stay Interview

1. What makes you come to work every day?
2. What about your job makes you want to jump out of bed?
3. What about your job makes you want to hit the snooze button?
4. What are you passionate about?
5. What is your dream job?
6. If you won the lottery and didn't have to work, what would you miss?
7. What did you love in your last position that you're not doing now?
8. If you had a magic wand, what would be the one thing you would change about your work, your role and your responsibilities?
9. What do you think about on your way to work?
10. What keeps you up at night about your job?
11. Have you ever thought of leaving? What made you consider it, and what made you stay?
12. How do you prefer we show appreciation to you?
13. Where do you see yourself in five years?
14. Can you describe a recent good day at work?
15. What about the company culture would you change?
16. What are we doing well as a company, and what could we improve?

---

2   Some of the questions in my list were derived from the following book, while others are my own: Kaye, Beverly, and Giulioni, Julie Winkle, *Help Them Grow or Watch Them Go*, Berrett-Koehler Publishers Inc., Oakland, CA, 2018, 2nd edition.

17. What can we do to best support you?

18. What can we do to make this a great place to work?

19. What would you like to change about your job, team or department?

20. Which of your talents are not being used in your current role?

21. What motivates or demotivates you?

22. What can I do as your manager to best support you?

———————

When closing an exit or stay interview, the manager or interviewer should not trivialize an employee's concerns or make excuses for the company.

———————

When closing an exit or stay interview, the manager or interviewer should not trivialize an employee's concerns or make excuses for the company. SHRM suggests repeating back to the employee some of the key points they stated and expressing your commitment to making your workplace a great place to work and to bring larger, company-wide issues to leadership's attention.[3]

Whether you choose to conduct exit interviews or stay interviews or both, that choice will enhance the valuable feedback that your employees give. Exit interviews and stay interviews complement one another. The key is to act on any pressing issues that are identified in the interviews. Be honest and transparent about what you can and cannot do to remedy any problem; don't over promise and under deliver.

Let me share one final story about a colleague we'll call Beth. Beth came to see me about her job and upward mobility in the company. She loved

———————

3   Society for Human Resource Management, "Stay Interview Questions," Resources and Tools and Samples, 2019.

the company and the people, but she was receiving offers to go work for our competitors. We discussed what the competitors offered her that she did not receive from her current employer. The competitors were offering her more money and a promotion, but the increase in salary would be used up in additional commuting costs (e.g., gasoline, wear and tear on her car), resulting in no pay increase for her. We discussed other promotional opportunities that she could pursue at her current company. She took advantage of these opportunities and was promoted. That employer retained her for another decade.

The workforce is full of employees like Marjorie and Beth — who will tell you the truth, if you bother to ask, and who can be retained if your timing and your attitude is right. The workforce is also full of employees who you are destined to lose, but whose insights as they depart can help your organization improve, if you'll take the time to listen. Organizations that consistently conduct exit and stay interviews — then act on the suggestions, recommendations and opportunities articulated by candid employees — see remarkable results. Try it at your company, and I bet you 'll see the results quickly: a decrease in employee turnover; improved processes, culture and relationships; and some of your star performers staying with the company longer than you hoped was even possible.

ABOUT THE AUTHOR

Michele Fantt Harris
SHRM-SCP, SPHR, ACC

Michele Fantt Harris is the Executive Vice President, Human Resources, for the National Cooperative Bank in Washington, D.C. A seasoned HR professional, Michele has worked in human resources in the education, nonprofit, healthcare, and the finance and insurance industries.

This is Michele's sixth professional human resources anthology: To read her previous books, check out *What's Next in Human Resources* (Greyden Press 2015), *Rethinking Human Resources* (Red Letter Publishing 2015), *Evolution of Human Resources* (Red Letter Publishing 2016), *Humans@Work* (Red Letter Publishing 2017) and *You@Work* (Silver Tree Publishing, 2018).[4]

Michele is active in many human resources organizations, and is past president of the Human Resources Association of the National Capital Area and the former Black Human Resources Network. She has been a member of the Society for Human Resource Management since 1985, served on the Society for Human Resource Management national board from 1996 through 2001 and is a past chair of the SHRM Foundation Board of Directors.

A member of the International Coach Federation, Michele is a Certified Career Management Coach (CCMC) through The Academies, Inc.

---

4   Books originally published by Red Letter Publishing became part of the Silver Tree Publishing catalog in 2017 through an asset acquisition.

Michele is a Certified Retirement Coach through Career Partners International. She is a member of the Retirement Coaches Association and is an author in the RCA's anthology, *The Retirement Challenge* (Retirement Coaches Association, 2018).

A member of Delta Sigma Theta Sorority, Inc., she served on the board of the Delta Research and Educational Foundation from 2008 to 2014. Michele currently serves on the Board of Regents for the Leadership Center for Excellence.

Michele received her Bachelor of Arts degree from the University of Maryland, Baltimore County; a Master of Administrative Science from Johns Hopkins University; and her Juris Doctorate from the University of Baltimore School of Law. A certified Senior Professional in Human Resources (SPHR) and SHRM-SCP, Michele teaches the SHRM Learning System at Prince Georges Community College and Catholic University.

Michele is a native of Baltimore, Maryland, and currently resides with her husband in the District of Columbia with their rescue Brittany Spaniel canine kid.

Learn more and contact Michele:

✉ MFHarris@ncb.coop
✉ Michele.Harris19@gmail.com

Chapter Three

DENISE JEROME

"It All Starts with Your Story"

As an entrepreneur, I believe that innovation is the key to success — that it is vital if we are to consistently survive and grow. Without innovation, companies will become complacent and die.

However, innovation does not magically happen. While innovation can be charted as a metric, the inspiration behind the innovation cannot be measured and tracked. It must be fostered. Inspiration has to be found. Inspiration occurs as a result of each person's personal story.

_____

I believe that our stories define who we are and what we want to achieve *or not achieve* in life. Stories inspire us.

_____

I believe that our stories define who we are and what we want to achieve *or not achieve* in life. Stories inspire us. They inspire us to either be satisfied with our current station in life or change it, in hopes of achieving the kind of results we've seen in *another* person's story.

We have traditionally thought of stories as whimsical and fictional. We rarely think about each person's individual story. But we each have a plot, setting, conflict, characters, theme and point of view. The workplace is a large part of any person's story. As employers, it is obviously a large part of our story too. Why would we not recognize this opportunity to blend our company's story with our team's stories and create new opportunities for us all?

Part of my story has to become part of my team's story. My goals for company growth must incorporate team growth. When they succeed, I succeed. It is not about me. It is about them. They have to become part of my story and I need to be part of theirs.

The success this process can bring in the form of innovation was demonstrated to me about four years ago. We had recently changed our name from The Catering Company to Michaelis Events. We were trying to enlarge our brand and were not sure how to proceed. We had traditionally been a caterer, and we wanted to expand into the world of total event management, inclusive of décor. One of my employees came from the interior décor world. We were not only struggling with how to change the mindset of our customer, but also our event team. They were not confident in selling our new services because they were not confident we could execute. We had to prove our capabilities on two fronts.

Kalye, one of our employees, was very imaginative and quite the visionary. She also had a passion for the Harry Potter brand. At that time, we managed a venue that was a renovated church and resembled the look of the great hall in the Harry Potter movies.

Kalye suggested we build our own signature event to demonstrate our capabilities at total event management. After all, we would have to provide all the design, planning, décor, food, rentals, on-site management, ticket sales, etc.

It was a huge task, but nonetheless a fantastic idea! We moved forward with the concept on a small scale and were amazed at the success the first year! We are now entering our fourth year and event management has grown to be a large revenue generator. It has even spurred a separate profit center that we call our Signature Series.

This innovative process blended Kalye's personal passions from her story with the company's overall strategies for success and growth. However, this story started with Kalye's passions. We took an element of her passion and created a greater purpose in our work, which presented an inspirational moment.

Innovation is the result of inspiration. Inspirations come from a person's passion and purpose in life. Stories are built around passion and purpose. Stories *are* a powerful tool!

Passion ⌐
        ├→ Inspiration → Innovation
Purpose ⌐

DISCOVERING PASSION AND PURPOSE

According to Christian Fisher in *How to Define Your Passion in Life*, "Passion can be anything that simultaneously challenges you, intrigues you and motivates you. Contrary to the idea that doing what you love makes work effortless, a **passion** puts you to work. It's what you're willing to sacrifice lesser leisure and pleasures for."[1]

I was raised Catholic my whole life. Because I am Catholic, we re-enact the "Passion of Jesus Christ" each year during Holy week prior to

---

1   Fisher, Christian, "How to Define Your Passion in Life?" Work - Chron.com, http://work.chron.com/define-passion-life-10132.html. Accessed 30 March 2019.

Easter. I always wondered why it was called "The Passion." That never made sense to me. I never associated it with the definition of the word passion before.

And while the story of his crucifixion is called the "Passion" because of the word's Latin root for "suffering," the entire life story of Jesus, as it was taught to me, definitely demonstrated what true passion is. Jesus's passion for his people was so strong that He was willing to sacrifice His life. He was motivated, willing and tireless in the service of others. Showing His love and dedication to His people was elevated above all else.

Imagine if you could extract a tiny fraction of that kind of passion in your everyday life. The results would be stupendous! Your accomplishments would be monumental!

So, what is your passion? What are you willing to sacrifice for your passion? How can you bring that back to the workplace? How do you elevate your team's passion while they are at work?

_____

What are you willing to sacrifice for your passion? How can you bring that back to the workplace? How do you elevate your team's passion while they are at work?

_____

Your **purpose** is what you decide to do with that passion. How do I channel that passion and get results?

An exercise that helped me discover my passion and purpose started with a simple listing of all the things I enjoy doing and that bring me fulfillment. They simply feel natural and good. My list included lifting up the spirits of others, solving problems, challenges that can be overcome within a given timeframe, being outdoors, new and unique places to visit, my family, honesty, authenticity, discovering how I can be the best person I was made to be.

From this list I discovered my purpose. It is to help others discover their self-worth, their potential. I enjoy and gravitate toward the individual who does not appear to realize their value in society. I gain a huge amount of satisfaction from fostering the individual who sees himself or herself with limited potential. I am a person of religious faith, who believes each one of us was born with a purpose. I welcome the opportunity to help others find that purpose.

Perhaps this would be a great exercise as an employer to bring into the workplace. Allow your team to discover their passion and purpose, and then encourage them to share it with you and others.

We have recently added this exercise to our team experiences. (I discuss the team experiences at the end of the chapter under "Innovative Company Ideas.") I have shared my story (which is told later in this chapter) with my team and invited them to share their story during the month they host the company team experience. It allows us to see who they are and why they chose the experience they did.

How does this relate to my team? Well if I don't know where my passion and purpose is, how can I expect to help others find their passion and purpose?

_____

As a person, I care for the individual. As an employer, I care about what this brings to the company mission.

_____

What do I care? As a person, I care for the individual. As an employer, I care about what this brings to the company mission.

One of the key training experiences at our company involves teaching our Event Consultants to learn about their customer. They should know what that person's story is and how it affects their event. We have actually built into our process a technique to discover what the top three priorities are for that customer. We ask this in the initial consultation and throughout the journey, especially at the final walk-through. We use this information to make each event personal. It helps us uncover the passion and purpose for their event.

This process should not be reserved for our customers; it should also be turned inward. As employers, we need to take the time to gain clarity about the story we want to tell to the world — to our customers, to our prospects and to our future employees. This story says who we are both personally and professionally. The story is the secret ingredient. In addition, this focus on brand story needs to translate down the chain to your key management. It encourages a sustainable culture, whether you are the entrepreneur or the manager.

In our business, we also decided to add our story to our employee manual, and we verbally tell the story during orientation. We want our new team members to see our failures and successes. We want them to understand we have been in their shoes.

We want our new team members to see our failures and successes. We want them to understand we have been in their shoes.

Passion and purpose are two key steps necessary to create inspirations. Inspirations lead to innovation in the workplace. So how do we get to inspiration?

DRAWING AIR INTO THE LUNGS

The literal definition of the word inspiration is the act of "drawing air into the lungs."[2] It is a feeling of enthusiasm that comes from your environment and gives new and creative ideas. As employers, how can we create an environment that encourages and incites these ideas? When our teams are inspired, how do we handle those ideas? How do we foster the growth of these inspirations without discouraging our teams when it might not be practical to act on each inspiration?

Matthew Kelly, author of *The Biggest Lie in the History of Christianity*, wrote "People don't do anything until they are inspired, but once they are inspired there is almost nothing they won't do ... Inspiration sets free our pent-up possibilities filling us with the boldness to live life to the fullest."[3] Imagine the fuel your company's innovation could run on with that philosophy!

Throughout our lives, we each have multiple points of inspiration. We get "clues" that are dropped into our paths and into our thoughts. The trick is how we choose to act on them. Are these moments viewed as inspiration or simply passing thoughts? Do we act or brush them off? Are we motivated by our passion and purpose or tempted by the tendency to ignore what our minds are trying to tell us? Does our "history" or our *individual story* compel us to move inspiration to action?

---

2   "Inspiration," *The American Heritage Medical Dictionary*, Houghton Mifflin Company, 2007, https://www.merriam-webster.com/dictionary/inspiration#other-words.

3   Kelly, Matthew, (2018). *The Biggest Lie in the History of Christianity*. North Palm Beach, FL. Eucalyptus Media Group.

INSPIRATION AT WORK, AND THE STORY BEHIND THE STORY

I believe that how we treat inspiration at work is as important as how we treat it in our personal lives. As employers, though, we may find ourselves challenged regarding how to motivate our employees to act on their inspirations so our companies' innovation machines can be fully functional. But the how is simple. *It all starts with their story!*

We have to build physical and cultural environments that encourage our teams to participate. If we boast that we care about our team's participation, but don't welcome ideas, new thought changes, or even personal adjustment, we really aren't sending the right message. How can we inspire people with truly authentic moments?

Many years ago, my personal story became one of my greatest gifts, even though I didn't recognize it then. My story was built on weak cornerstones. I operated often from a place of greed and pride. Not surprisingly then, when my original business forecast fell short, my personal and business finances became jeopardized. But it was my pride that nearly destroyed me.

———————

Many years ago, my personal story became one of my greatest gifts, even though I didn't recognize it then.

———————

I had always been a hard worker, a loyal Christian — someone who maintained high morals, great family ethics and, over all, endeavored to be a model citizen and a good human being. I was always the good girl, the easy child. I had been raised on the premise that hard work paid off. I graduated fourth in my high school class and had an overall GPA in college of 3.6. I considered myself intelligent. I am, by no means, brilliant but I am a seeker of truth and answers. If I don't know the answer, I know how to find it.

Our current business, Michaelis Events, was founded on a different philosophy than our original business, EuroMarket. Our product offering today is not what we intended 19 years ago. I had never failed at any undertaking that I can remember. Failure was simply not a word in my vocabulary. However, when our business didn't go as planned, despite diligent efforts, research, hard work and financial sacrifice, we had to make some tough decisions.

Asking for help was something I was not accustomed to doing. In fact, I was often the person who helped others in my family, not the reverse. I had always considered myself the leader and caretaker. Having to ask my family and friends for help was a huge blow to my pride. It nearly depressed me. It put me on a spiraling path downward, and an emotional journey that I was too embarrassed to talk about with others. In my mind, I had failed. I had reached the point of "worst case scenario." I was throwing myself my own private pity party and it stung.

I can't possibly expect others to trust in me and share their stories, so I can learn how to incite inspiration in the workplace, if I won't share my story first.

Why would I share this now? What possible impact could this have on building inspiration in the workplace? The answer is this: I can't possibly expect others to trust in me and share their stories, so I can learn how to incite inspiration in the workplace, if I won't share my story first. Telling my story — my perceived shame, what I viewed as my personal failure — made me human to them. I was no longer just the employer. I was the person who had experienced pain and suffering like they had.

I demonstrated authenticity, transparency and inspiration to my team by telling them my story. My worst experience became my best gift.

This was not an easy task. This was an emotional journey. I am not a "touchy-feely" person. I am normally very private with my struggles, but I *had* to share to prove myself to them.

Contrary to my initial belief that telling my story to my employees might be met with disgust, pity, shame, and multiple other negative reactions, the opposite actual happened. A connection was formed. People realized they were not alone on their personal journey. I realized *I* was not alone. My team now became part of my story. Their purpose began to include growth of the company for success. They felt they were an essential piece of the journey to achieve success.

STORY-BASED, INSPIRED CULTURES ... EVERY DAY

So, we had now included our team in our story. And perhaps you have done likewise at your organization. We have walked through the tough times and now share in the success of good times. We have demonstrated their value to us. They know, without a doubt, that we care about their stories. We have invited them into our story. Now, how can we allow them to be inspired in the workplace, by our collective stories, and yet maintain individuality?

This is a difficult task. Being real and authentic is not always easy. Some days, we are each so wrapped up in our personal life and struggles that it's difficult to be open to others — to be leaders and listeners.

Recently, while visiting my father in Vero Beach, FL, I visited the St. Helen's Church. The reading that day was about how we criticize others. We mock the proverbial wood splinter in another's eye when we, in fact, don't recognize the log in our own.

The priest's homily that day focused on hypocrisy. The origins of the word "hypocrite" refer to a theatrical mask from the 1st century B.C.E.[4] The priest suggested that we all wear this mask. We all portray on the outside what our mask is. However, without the mask, we are not always that person we pretend to be. He said it's okay to wear this mask. As a priest, he wears his mask each day too. However, we should all remember that it is just that — a mask. We must be sure not to lie to ourselves. We must always be grounded in the truth!

As leaders, we too often wear masks. It is not always deliberate. I know that I often really don't care, at that precise moment, what went wrong in someone else's life yesterday. Timing is often a factor. My agenda or my own personal circumstances are often a major distraction. Yet I will sit down to listen even though my inner side is calling me to be somewhere else. It is okay to make that sacrifice without an intentional heart. Just be sure to understand it is only that and not pat yourself on the back for "doing the right thing."

FINDING INSPIRATION AS A PRACTICAL MATTER

Getting (and staying) inspired is a practice, and it takes work. I enjoy using books and articles to inspire my own thinking, and I'm sharing several ideas you might consider when finding inspiration as a practical matter in your career and organization. Find what works for you and your team, and capitalize on it. Each plan will look different.

---

4   "Hypocrite," *Merriam Webster Dictionary*, https://www.merriam-webster.com/words-at-play/hypocrite-meaning-origin.

- **Devotional/Inspirational Readings**

  – **Personal:** Get a daily devotional and read it at a designated time each day. I like to read it in the morning after my shower. It sets my thoughts in a positive light for the day. I enjoy *Jesus Calling* by Sarah Young, my husband reads *Your Best Life* by Joel Osteen, and many people sign up for an online devotional that is sent to your email each day.

  – **Business:** Post new inspirational sayings in designated places each day/week/month. Perhaps try to demonstrate or incorporate the inspirations in your daily/weekly/monthly "huddles."

- **Explore a New Hobby**

  – **Personal:** Try a new hobby or sport. Play with a friend or join a team or club to *make* a new friend.

  – **Business:** Get your co-workers to develop a team and join a recreational or competitive league. Virtual or fantasy leagues can also be formed in-house to foster team spirit.

- **Read Books/Listen to Podcasts & Playlists**

  – **Personal:** Try reading or listening to inspirational books. We all need constant uplifting.

  – **Business:** Read a book as a team. Make sure the book is something you can develop and work on together for a new process or improvement in the business.

- **Outside Your Comfort Zone**

  – **Personal:** Do something you don't normally do. It can be as simple as volunteering, or as daring as flying in a two-man WWII plane (that would be me!). Share your worst life experience. Let others be part of your story.

  – **Business:** Volunteer to lead instead of just participating on a board. Develop ideas that push your team outside of their comfort zone. They need to be constantly challenged to be more than they are.

- **Journal**
  - **Personal:** My husband and I attended a marriage encounter weekend to "refresh" our marriage after 33 years. This experience encourages journaling thoughts. I was amazed at how much more you can convey with words on paper rather than just speaking thoughts aloud.
  - **Business:** Have your team journal on a specific topic in meetings. Allow only two minutes to journal. Discuss the results and be open. You may be surprised at the outcome!

- **Display Quotes/Images**
  - **Personal:** Place items around you that inspire you. Pictures at home, on your phone and computer screens, special sayings, goal sheets, etc.
  - **Business:** Allow your team to decorate their workspace with what inspires them. Give them the freedom to be creative. Our team wanted to design stations to go around our commissary/kitchen area that reflected our company core values and certain tools they needed consistency on. They proposed we have a "paint" day where the team participated and actually painted their area. It was a great team bonding experience and the result is a conversation starter for guests who visit our facility.

- **Join a New "Insight" Group**
  - **Personal:** Join a Bible study, finance class, family class, etc. — something that might be considered a "self-improvement" group.
  - **Business:** Join a CEO group (like Vistage), a peer group (like NAWBO), or a local business community group (like a Chamber). Join a group that will provide insight for your role in the company, challenge your existing thinking, re-enforce

positive choices and assist with unfamiliar territory. You might even be surprised with an unexpected connection. As for offering new insights to your entire team, there are many ways to translate what works in the personal realm to the business world. For example, we offer Dave Ramsey money-management classes once per year to all of our employees, and now open it up to anyone on our mailing list who wants to attend.

TRANSITIONING INSPIRATION TO INNOVATION

To be an effective leader, you have to be about your team, not yourself. People follow authentic, selfless leadership. People aspire to others who they believe will give them hope and inspiration.

Assuming we have chosen our teams wisely and we have the right person in the right "seat on the bus," as they say, how do we build a sense of family in the workplace? How do we encourage and foster inspiration? If a team member's personal life is not right, their mind will always be somewhere else. How do we engage them at work? How do we pull from their personal story, discover their passions and allow them an escape from other conflicts in their story? Perhaps the workplace can become their "safe place" when other parts of their life may not be going well. How can we break through and have them participate at work?

The Eight Essentials of Innovation by McKinsey argues that there is no silver bullet — that it's all about strategy. The article outlines steps for achieving innovation, in this order: inspire, choose, discover, evolve, accelerate, scale, extend and mobilize. The main message is this: if your company's product, process or business model is not revolutionized on a periodic basis, your company will fold.[5] As a leader, you must drive innovation or your company's existence will be pointless.

_____

As a leader, you must drive innovation or your company's existence will be pointless.

_____

As employers and leaders, we have the ability to act on all of these steps. However, I would like to specifically address the first two steps: inspire and choose.

It all starts with "*inspire,*" which brings us back to how we create and motivate to gain this end product. Earlier in this chapter, I briefly referenced my personal story and how my perceived failure actually turned out to be a great gift. Because of this gift, I actually learned to recognize the difference between true failure and enlightenment. I would define failure as the choice to not try something you actually were inspired to do. It is not failure if you fall. It is failure if you choose to not get back up. I would define enlightenment as the awakening of inspiration to further our journey to be the best person we can be.

When my husband and I opened the doors for our business on March 1, 2000, we were nervous, scared, exhausted, thrilled, exhilarated, accomplished and proud all at the same time. We had a dream that we had dared to make happen.

Our dream was a small specialty store with a deli in the back, specialty wines and lots of personality, hence the name "EuroMarket." We had a vision of multiple stores, with great employee ideas and incentives, strong vendor relationships, and a family dynamic that would extend

_____

5   "The Eight Essentials of Innovation," *McKinsey Insights*, McKinsey & Company, April 2015.

beyond our literal family to our staff, vendors, customers and others. We had done so much research and invested so much time and money. We had two partners with minority ownership who felt we had great potential, and they invested a sizable amount of money, two different times. The bank thought we had a solid plan. We leveraged everything we owned. We went into the venture debt free, other than our mortgage. We had been married 15 years, with two daughters who were 13 and 10 at the time. This was the perfect time to start this venture. We thought we had structured it all for success.

———————

This was the perfect time to start this venture. We thought we had structured it all for success. Then our great adventure turned into our great disaster.

———————

Seven months later, the momentum we started to gain was losing pace. I discovered I was pregnant with baby number three. Cash flow was tight. I was borrowing from Peter to pay Paul.

By February of 2001, we knew we were in trouble. We were quickly moving to our worst-case scenario. We were going to have to sell our house. Our debt was increasing rapidly and we knew we had to go into survival mode. Our great adventure had turned into our great disaster. We had to ask our family for help. This was a huge embarrassment for me personally. I had always been the leader ... the one who was on her way ... determined ... accomplished. I was now publicly humiliated. I was so prideful that I couldn't even ask my brother for help. My husband had to do it.

In July 2001, we sold our house and moved into my brother's basement with a teenager, a pre-adolescent and a new baby. My brother and sister-in-law had a teenager and two small children of their own. Ten people under one roof. My family never even hesitated to help. They didn't even think about it. They just said yes.

It became clear that we had to re-invent our business. We are not, and we were not, quitters. We are survivors. I was determined that I would pay back every cent I had borrowed. No one else needed to sacrifice for my bad decisions. My motivation was now not for me; it was to clear my name. I associated repayment of debt with my success and legacy.

I began to listen to my customers. I began to listen to my team. We looked at where our success was and began to grow that area. We started a new business sector, focused on catering, and created a DBA "The Catering Company." We eliminated inventory. We eliminated some of our square footage to decrease rent. We brought our oldest daughter in to generate sales. We eliminated the retail portion. We made a lot of tough decisions.

Nineteen years later and many other lessons learned, we are growing and surviving. We are now a full-service events experience company. We rebranded again, expanded and did a full name change to Michaelis Events. We are still happily married. We have raised three daughters, two who are now married and mothers. Our youngest is heading to college this year.

NEVER GIVE UP

So many lessons were learned, but there is one lesson that stands out above them all. Many years ago, when we were first thinking about starting our business, a wise and seasoned business man gave me some sound advice. He told me that it would always be tough. That it never gets easy. But that I should never, never, never give up! I kept that with me. I never realized how often I would need to apply that lesson, but it is the simplest and most honest piece of advice I could ever use consistently.

There is only one reason we were successful with this advice. It is called innovation. You cannot grow if you stand still. Inspiration has to sustain us to reach our goals. Ideas are just ideas. Inspiration creates and drives innovation.

_____

Ideas are just ideas. Inspiration creates and drives innovation.

_____

As I mentioned before, there is no silver bullet. We made several key business decisions that included hiring a more skilled labor force, providing better training, rebranding our business and simplifying our product concept. These are good business practices for growing companies. Solid business practices are necessary for survival.

Innovation involves a broader concept. It is not only the ability to incorporate good business practices, but it is the ability to be able to recognize potential new avenues for your business to explore. For example, our business began as a retail specialty market. It was re-engineered into a catering commissary, which then grew to an events company, which has matured into an events experience company. Our events experience company has developed its own line of signature events, like a Wizard's Extravaganza and Pop-Up Chef dinners, and full event management. We have looked outside our company and reinvented ourselves consistently so that we are always ahead of our competition.

Remember McKinsey's innovation steps — first inspire, then choose? That second step is the most important. Choosing refers to a company's responsibility to make good decisions and its ability to manage risks. Not all inspirations will be insightful ideas. As leaders, we must systematically gut-check all ideas to see if they truly are in line with our core values, mission, and company direction.

I would take this second step further. Innovation in the workplace is an individual choice as much as a company choice. We cannot force people to be part of our process, share their stories, make us part of their passion and purpose, and be open to inspiration. It is a choice. It is as much a choice on the part of the employee as the employer. As a company grows and becomes more innovative, the culture will change as well. People will think differently. All teams and leadership will be held accountable for process improvements, quality products and processes, efficiency, culture in the workplace, core value adherence and financial results. While a team member might have proved to be a valuable part in the beginning, their lack of involvement in future growth may now become a hindrance if they are resistant to change. As the company grows and becomes more innovative, the culture may no longer be a good fit for each person. Accountability is imperative and excuses cannot be allowed to inhibit success.

————————

We cannot force people to be part of our process, share their stories, make us part of their passion and purpose, and be open to inspiration. It is a choice.

————————

This is one of the toughest decisions an employer has to make—deciding when it is time for an employee to leave. We have asked to be part of that person's story and invited them into our story. They are now family. But sometimes people who we enthusiastically hired cannot or will not share the collective vision anymore, cannot be inspired and innovative in the way we need for them to be.

I remember my mother telling me when I was younger that she didn't raise us to stay at home with her. She raised us to be responsible adults who played a part in the world. She said that as we grow, we may disagree with the house rules or choose to simply not obey them anymore. That was okay. However, that meant it was time to be out on our own.

There is simple wisdom in this statement that can be applied to the workplace. If a team member chooses to not follow our "family rules" or thinks they are "outside of the rules," then it is time for them to move on. It doesn't mean we don't value them or like them anymore. It just means they have stopped choosing to participate in our family/organizational rules. They have chosen to move on.

INNOVATIVE COMPANY IDEAS

- **Create a position in your company that is actually titled "Innovation Engineer," "Visionary," or something similar.** As a company, we decided that if we were actually going to lead in our industry, we had to be on the cutting edge. We had to always be charting our course in blue waters (sailing ahead of our competition), not red waters (swimming with the sharks). Depending upon the size of *your* company, this innovation or visionary position can be a full-time position or incorporated with another position. However, it has to be measurable.

- **Develop a monthly team experience.** One of our team leaders developed this idea. Because our company is all about the experience and the story, she suggested we have each employee take a month and develop a team experience that is representative of their individual story. At first, team members were hesitant. However, now they are volunteering on their own.

  Once a month, we mandate one hour that all team members must participate in the activity. Only upper management

and the activity leader know exactly what the activity is.
Other team members are simply told what time to show up
and what to wear.

Some examples of these unique activities are:

— Building gingerbread houses

— Crafting

— Team company trivia contest

— Pilates/yoga

— Nerf gun fights

— Video game competition

— Writing letters to our service men/women abroad

- **Company transparency.** At our monthly meetings, we share where
we are with our finances. We develop our profit & loss statement
for each month according to the scale of $1. We have separate
jars with set categories we want to track each month. We base the
P&L on a penny scale. A different employee divides the pennies up
each month and has to explain what the category entails (like fixed
expenses, wages, advertising, inventory, etc.). We even have a jar for
the bank. If there is a loss on the month, money comes from the
bank. It makes a huge impact on the employees to see their wages are
still paid even though the company had a loss that month.

- **Benchmarking and collaborating with other companies.** Part
of our Visionary's role is to help all departments gain inspiration
through collaborating with companies outside our industry segment.
For example, we visited with a construction company to gain insight
about project management. This gave our newly created project
management department insight for establishing procedures. We
are not competing industries, but we can gain a lot of insight from
experienced leaders. We are working with several other companies

for new products developed, new sales techniques, new décor options and more.

IT IS ALWAYS A CHOICE

Life is full of choices at home and at work. Nothing is ever forced. Choice is a gift.

As leaders and employers, we can choose to innovate. We can choose to share our stories, encourage others to share their stories, and invite others into our story, hoping it will incite passion, purpose, inspiration and ultimately innovation. However, we cannot force others to do this, nor can we choose for them. As an employer, you must decide when the effort on your end outweighs the benefits.

As leaders and employers, we can choose to innovate. We can choose to share our stories, encourage others to share their stories, and invite others into our story, hoping it will incite passion, purpose, inspiration and ultimately innovation.

Do you find yourself making excuses for lack of achievement in your company or life? It is always normal to yearn for more because we are built for more. However, are you standing still, waiting for life to happen to you? Do you let the fear of failure stop you from growing? From innovating? If we completely eliminate the company view for innovation, do you realize that innovation must start with you personally each and every day? How can you demonstrate by example or expect your team to go outside their boundaries if you don't?

Company leaders, in particular, have a choice to make. We must ask ourselves: "Do we innovate, change and grow *or* do we stand still and fold?" There are really only two options. I believe that as leaders and employers, we lead by example. What choice will you make?

ABOUT THE AUTHOR

Denise Jerome

As a successful entrepreneur of 19 years (employing mostly women), the Past President of NAWBO Kentucky, and a mother of three successful daughters, Denise Jerome understands the challenges associated with innovation and inspiration in companies of all sizes. Her comprehensive approach to elevating both the person and the company stems from years of experience with her own company's challenges and her previous employment in corporate America, where she advanced in her field, even as a minority among her peers.

Denise believes that our environment, beliefs, encouragement and continual development of a person's story can foster an atmosphere that will stimulate innovation. Innovation challenges status quo and increases the likelihood of future success and endurance in any company. The trick is to invest in your team's individual stories, discover what motivates them, and then weave that motivation into your company's story to create inspiration and grow success.

The reinvention of Denise's founding company, Michaelis Events, is a testimony to her ingenuity, determination, and foresight to build and grow innovation in the face of adversity. She enjoys lifting all team members, learning what truly motivates them, and blending that motivation into a common goal that benefits both the person and the company.

Denise earned two Bachelor's degrees, in biology and chemistry, and enjoys a life of adventure and outdoor fun. She and her husband of 34 years, Robbie, reside in Crestwood, Kentucky, and have raised three strong-willed and independent daughters, and are now grandparents to five grandsons.

Learn more and contact Denise:

✉ DJerome@MyMEStory.com
in LinkedIn.com/in/DeniseJeromeCEO
📞 502-243-0000

Chapter four

LISA M. JOHNSON

"Managing Compliance with Confident Communications"

Imagine it is a typical day at your job. You are hard at work, trying to meet your managerial goals for the day while juggling the various, inevitable interruptions. Suddenly, your focus is broken by a very different type of distraction outside your office window. It is the flashing blue lights of a police car as it pulls up to the front of your company's building. *What is going on?* There is an immediate hum in the air as nearby employees stop what they are doing and start asking the question out loud. You walk into the hall to see heads peeking out of their office doors, everyone staring at each other wide-eyed. Being experienced in your role, you automatically go into "manager mode" and advise everyone to stay calm and to stay put at their work areas.

You see the General Manager (GM) head to the front entrance to meet two police officers. After a brief, inaudible conversation, the GM walks away and returns a few minutes later with a representative from Human Resources and one of your fellow department managers, Frank, at his side. Walking past employees who are now frozen in place, they approach the police officers. They talk to Frank and he is then handcuffed and quietly led to the police car, lights still flashing. The officers drive away with Frank in the back seat.

What just happened? You make your way to the GM, who recounts how the police received a complaint of assault against Frank, filed by another employee. *Assault? No Way!* Frank is one of the most even-keeled, well-meaning managers you have had the pleasure to work with. Through eyewitness accounts from different employees, the details of what happened start to emerge. The evening prior, Frank was verbally counseling an employee. During the conversation, Frank put his hand on the employee's shoulder, gave it a squeeze and a shake. Witnesses perceived it to be a gesture of encouragement but the employee, who had received recent corrective action from Frank for performance, called the police to make an allegation of assault. Frank remained behind bars until his wife could arrive to pay the cash bail.

How did it come to this? You are stunned, unable to fathom how their relationship reached this point. For the remainder of the day, you somehow manage to compartmentalize. You stay focused on tasks, don't pass judgement, don't play attorney. You know that employees are watching you and, as a department manager, they will follow your actions, not your words.

In the midst of a workplace crisis, you have to compartmentalize. You stay focused on tasks, don't pass judgement, don't play attorney. You know that employees are watching you and, as a department manager, they will follow your actions, not your words.

At the end of the day, when you finally have privacy, a flood of emotions overtake you. Anger — *Frank did not deserve this!* Confusion — *What am I missing, what drove the employee to take such an extreme measure?* Fear and helplessness — *If this can happen to a supervisor like Frank, what prevents it from happening to me?*

MANAGING EMPLOYEE RELATIONS WITH CONFIDENCE AND COMPLIANCE

Frank's story is not fiction. The hypothetical scenario I have painted for you is based on a true story. And while it was surely one of the more harrowing experiences I've had in my 25+ years as a human resources professional, I can recall numerous other unpleasant examples involving a manager in the course of their job. What I have learned from these difficult experiences can perhaps be instructive to you as well. And the core lesson is this: No matter how busy we are serving customers or bosses or the bottom line, we must never lose sight of proactive and persistent attention to employee relations. The vast majority of managers are not equipped to effectively deal with day-to-day employee relations issues. And it's in the daily (and arguably mundane) interactions where serious issues can take root.

———————

No matter how busy we are serving customers or bosses or the bottom line, we must never lose sight of proactive and persistent attention to employee relations.

———————

So how can we, as managers, oversee employee relations with confidence, compassion and compliance (for the law, for your company's employee bylaws, and for the ethical standards of your organization's culture)? It's no small order.

It starts with rethinking our roles as managers. The role of manager is a pivotal one and an increasingly demanding one. Managers must have strong technical skills to meet aggressive operational goals. Often, they have little or no participation in creating the goals and budgets to which they must adhere. Yet, much of their accomplishments are based on their ability to achieve these goals through their subordinates, which requires a very different set of skills. Additionally, good managers are called upon to participate in projects, and they wear many hats. Now factor in contemporary challenges they face, such as the changing workforce, global competition, and social media. And let's not omit the nature of today's litigious society, where legal advice for employees to sue their employer is advertised everywhere, at all hours.

⚠ **In a 2015 survey of 22,000 employees, managers reported symptoms of depression 6% higher than blue-collar workers and executives.**[1]

⚠ **In a 2014 survey of over 320,000 employees, when it comes to job satisfaction managers fall in the bottom 5%.**[2]

The article citing the survey goes on to present solutions, such as reducing administrative burden, reducing time in meetings and continuing professional development.[3] These outcomes are familiar to me. In one of the training seminars I facilitate with managers, one of the first things we do is take time to discuss reasons why it is a struggle for many managers to effectively handle employee performance issues. Some responses can be counted on to appear in practically every session:

- Lack of training
- Lack of simplicity

---

1   Wilkie, Dana, "The Miserable Middle Managers," *Society for Human Resource Management Blog*, March 12, 2018.

2   *Ibid.*

3   *Ibid.*

- Lack of time or competing priorities
- Personal tendency to be averse to difficult conversations.

There are distinct similarities between the solutions presented in the article about the high level of job dissatisfaction among managers and the reasons offered in the seminars about why they grapple with managing employee compliance.

FEAR, COMMUNICATION AND THE ROLE OF HR

There's another reason that goes unspoken and is key for why managers shy away from their responsibility to manage employee performance: they fear retaliation from a vindictive employee and, furthermore, worry they may not be supported by their employer if that happens. This is a sensitive issue and often goes unspoken because 1) they don't want others to perceive they lack confidence in their ability to lead and 2) they realize the questions it raises about their level of trust in their employer. I don't hear it in seminars but it surfaces in exit interviews, surveys and "off line" conversations.

I had been working at a global company with Mark, a regional manager, for about a year when we had such a conversation. Mark and I had a good working relationship, and he frequently requested HR assistance. I had noticed he rarely delivered corrective action without HR involvement, even lower-level actions. He was vocal about how much he valued the HR function. During employee training sessions, a lot of his statements included "HR says …" Over dinner the evening prior to an employee training event, I asked Mark specifically about his reliance on HR. He paused and explained that he gets very little pushback from his employees and even from his bosses when they know he has engaged HR while addressing issues. It frees him up to pay attention to the business side of his job that demands his attention, and he has the comfort of knowing that should there be an issue with an employee, his bases are covered. I told him I understood. I was not surprised by Mark's answer. I was grateful for his honesty and appreciative that he chose over-reliance on HR rather than avoidance.

However, Mark's solution is not a sustainable situation for most HR functions, including mine. Most organizations are not set up to provide that level of HR support to managers. We know a critical piece of the manager role is the ability to manage subordinates. What is not inherent is how effectively and confidently they accomplish it.

Imagine a workplace where you have communication skills that empower you to manage employee performance before they get out of your control. To handle yourself with poise under difficult employee situations. Where you feel confident that you aren't saying or doing something that will land you in legal trouble. And if you *are* named in a dispute, you are re-assured you have done the necessary things to minimize your exposure and the company's exposure. Wouldn't that be an awesome improvement to your work environment?

Is the answer to deliver more leadership development training? Research shows that companies around the world are spending billions of dollars on such training, including interpersonal skills such as communication.[4] Yet research also shows companies are not getting the expected return on investment (ROI) from their efforts.[5] Leadership development continues to be a number-one employer concern, with companies admitting they lack enough leaders with the right capabilities. Communication remains at the top of the list of those concerns.

---

4   Cochrane, Ryan, "How the World Spent $359 Billion on Training," *Administrate*, April 27, 2017.

5   McKinsey & Company, *Why Leadership Development Programs Fail*, January 2014.

⚠ **US Companies alone spend almost $14 billion annually on leadership development.**[6]

⚠ **It is estimated that 80% of work-related problems are related to communications issues.**[7]

So, delivering more training is not, by itself, the best answer. A CEO with whom I had the pleasure to work referred to it as "the big, costly, vanilla training." Just because a training program is expensive and glossy and looks impressive in a photo doesn't make it effective in developing your communication skills and other leadership attributes. Over the years, I have trained with thousands of managers and, from those experiences, I have discovered that three tried-and-true traits set effective leadership development training programs apart from the rest. These three common traits can help you realize the goal you imagined — to communicate with confidence when dealing with sticky employee relations matters.

Just because a training program is expensive and glossy and looks impressive in a photo doesn't make it effective in developing your communication skills and other leadership attributes.

---

1. Genuine Senior Leadership Support

The cost to companies of not doing anything to support leadership development is very high. A 2016 Gallup poll found that the majority of managers aren't proficient at leading people and that this lack of

---

6   *Ibid.*

7   The Cegos Group, "The Major Learning Trends and Indicators for 2013 and Beyond within the Asia Pacific Region," 2012, https://www.slideshare.net/JeremyBlain/cegos-learning-learner-trends-for-apac-2013-full-report.

leadership capability costs US corporations up to $550 billion annually.[8] And the EEOC reported it secured $505 million in settlements from employers in fiscal year 2018 for victims of discrimination. This is an increase from the previous year, when $398 million was secured in litigation or settlement.[9] It is well worth the effort for employers to invest in training for managers with the goal of sustained improvement of compliance culture.

The cost to companies of implementing a program without genuine senior leadership support is also very high. This is why I recommend the CEOs and HR professionals who hire me to go through the training prior to their employees. Managers know when members of the leadership team are not on board with programs. Those members either stay silent or, worse, undermine by conducting "business as usual" that is counter to the message the training program just delivered.

I recall having dinner with a group of managers prior to a training event that was part of an ongoing training program about company values, with a specific highlight on respect. They confided in me that their senior leader had recently visited for a business update and proceeded to humiliate their Division VP in front of them. They were uncomfortable for the Division VP but, more importantly, they took away the message that there isn't a full commitment to the company values. The training program became a "check the box" exercise with no real impact to company culture or compliance. Genuine senior leadership support means *all* members are aligned about the necessity of the training program, actively promoting it by encouraging participation and modeling the behaviors.

---

8   Hougaard, Rasmus, "The Real Crisis in Leadership," *Forbes*, September 9, 2018

9   Equal Employment Opportunity Commission, "EEOC Releases Fiscal Year 2018 Enforcement and Litigation Data," EEOC.gov, April 10, 2019.

Genuine senior leadership support means *all* members are aligned about the necessity of the training program, actively promoting it by encouraging participation and modeling the behaviors.

---

2. Practice Using Real-Life Examples

Knowledge retention comes with practice, so if you practice using real-life examples, you are much more likely to confidently apply what you have learned when the appropriate time comes. An admired former colleague of mine often used the phrase "Practice Makes Permanent." I use that phrase all the time, because I have found it to be true in my training workshops. One of the best ways to build confidence in communication is to provide a training workshop where time is allowed for managers to imagine how they should act in a real-life scenario, script what they would say and then role play it. It doubles the training time (for example, it takes what currently would be a two-hour training to a four-hour training investment) and it's well worth it. It is not an unreasonable expense, by any stretch, when you consider the costs of not training or not implementing effectively.

You may be familiar with the 70-20-10 model for effective learning.[10]

---

10 "The 70-20-10 Model for Learning and Development," developed by Morgan McCall, Michael M Lombardo and Robert A Eichinger and the Centre for Creative Leadership, Greensboro, NC. 1980s.

EFFECTIVE LEARNING

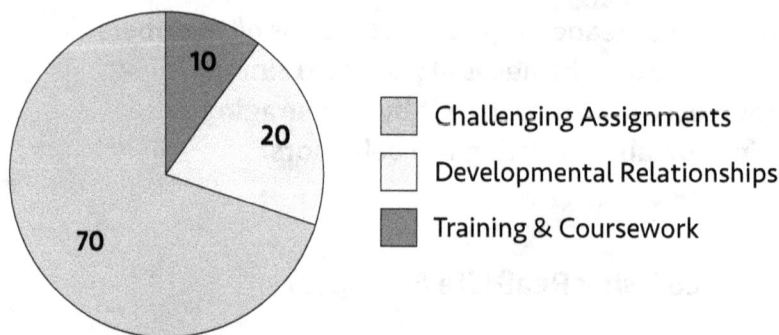

As a certified trainer, I prefer to use programs that subscribe to the 70-20-10 model when facilitating leadership development programs. On one occasion, when I was an HR leader inside a Fortune 500 company, I was delivering Achieve Forum's 2-day workshop entitled "Coaching Others for Top Performance" with a group of 20 managers. They came together for this event via an invitation from their senior leader, which laid out the purpose of the training. The senior leader copied the manager's boss and me. Arnold was one of the attendees at this particular session, and I had not met him prior to this event. He sat in the front row, arms crossed with a doubtful expression. I should mention that Arnold made a very imposing presence — he was a big guy. I mentally noted my challenge was to win Arnold over. The teaching material was very good, but it was the real-life discussion and role play that got the job done. Before the end of the first day, Arnold was actively participating and he let me know that he was looking forward to day two. The Achieve Forum leadership training program is one that gets high ratings because it offers the training event where there is instruction, the opportunity to network and learn from others, and the opportunity to practice real-life situations that can be applied on the job immediately. The result is empowered managers — it is the type of training that is worth the investment.

3. Follow Through

_____

An organization that has taken the time, effort and money to implement a compliance-related training program can find it is for nothing if there is no follow-through.

_____

An organization that has taken the time, effort and money to implement a compliance-related training program can find it is for nothing if there is no follow-through. True leaders will continue to apply the good learning techniques regardless, but the typical manager will find it easier to revert back to their old routine rather than experience the discomfort that comes with applying their newly practiced skills. That is, unless the organization has in place a plan, including:

- Training evaluation surveys
- Track metrics associated with the topic
- The attending manager's boss meets with the manager after the training to discuss the new communication skills they have learned and will be applying
- The attending manager's boss periodically asks "how is it going?" and get examples of the new communication skills applied
- Progress update on formal performance review
- Brief refresher program to reinforce learning and discuss challenges for script and role play.

A strong commitment to follow-through will address company concerns about ROI. You can track progress and make adjustments based on the data you accumulate.

FIRST, KNOW YOURSELF

Once you have completed training, you should apply the skills you have practiced as soon as possible. As you prepare, the more honest you are with yourself and the more you can "own" your actions, the more others will be honest and own theirs. It is not easy to be self-aware. I was leading a seminar for first-time managers and it became clear that Carla was struggling in her new role. Each time I introduced a new topic, Carla wanted to share her experience and none of them were positive. Whether it was her boss, a subordinate or a colleague, the problem — in her mind — lay elsewhere.

At one point, Carla re-enacted a conversation she had with an employee regarding the scheduling of work hours. I noted her statements began with "*You* don't realize …" and "If *you* worked as hard as I did …" and similar phrases intended to prove her points. I asked Carla if she felt she successfully conveyed her message and whether it made her feel better. She agreed that it did. Then I explained that her message may not have reached the employee in a way that would inspire change, which is what she really wanted. The employee was likely hearing the negative tone and words. When I repeated Carla's words back to her, an expression of realization dawned on her face. She smiled and acknowledged she needed to work on practicing her approach.

Before you expect others to respond, you should be self-aware. Here is a self-check list based upon a mix of learning and experience that has helped me, and that I use to help others. What follows is an in-depth discussion of the crucial steps in the self-awareness checklist.

BETTER COMMUNICATION FOR BETTER COMPLIANCE

Self Checklist

☐ Have I set expectations?

☐ Have I explained why?

☐ Am I walking the talk?

☐ Am I responding timely?

☐ Am I approaching with respect?

☐ Am I listening?

☐ Am I prepared?

☐ Am I offering encouragement?

☐ Do I have a documented Go-Forward Plan?

☐ Am I reinforcing?

Have You Set Expectations? And have you done so not just in your mind but in the mind of the person you have spoken with? Asking them to paraphrase what they heard is a good technique. I remember once I was meeting with a union steward and an employee returning to work from a suspension. I took time to counsel the employee about expectations going forward and I thought I had done a good job. When I finished, I asked him if he understood, and he turned to the union steward with a dubious expression. The union steward proceeded to say, "What Ms. Johnson is saying is …" And he neatly repeated what I had just said in 1/3 of the time and far fewer syllables than it took me. I think my mouth physically dropped open, I was that incredulous. *Was I that out of touch* *with my audience?* I had a good laugh with the union steward about it later; it was an eye-opening moment.

Have You Explained Why? The importance of explaining why is well documented. When people understand the reason for your position, it helps them buy into your vision. They see where their contribution fits into your goal. They feel valued. I attended a seminar once about giving recognition and it challenged attendees to not only thank someone but to "explain why," the piece that is often omitted. I tried it when I received a report from our payroll clerk. I said, "Laura, thank you for this report. Because you provided it so timely, I am going to be able to use it for my meeting in the morning and it will help me resolve a grievance." She responded, "You're welcome," which I anticipated. But before I hung up, she added, "You know, there are several other types of report I can run." And she proceeded to give me examples. I did not expect that! I have been "explaining why" since that seminar.

Are You Walking the Talk? A brief but hard-hitting book that helped me during my early years as a personnel clerk is *The Super Supervisor* by Mildred Ramsey. One of the chapters was titled "Don't Be a Hypocrite."[11] A hypocritical manager causes resentment that they may not realize. I worked with a senior manager who was strict about promptness with his team, but who was regularly late to meetings himself. Whether it was for interviews with job applicants or appointments with internal employees, he was chronically late, up to as much as 45 minutes. Eventually, complaints were made to his boss, which resulted in counseling but the damage was done. Employees were critical and found fault in other areas, such as his grand travel habits while he held the team to budget constraints. The senior manager's credibility eroded. If you find yourself engaging in hypocritical behavior, you should make changes.

---

11 Ramsey, Mildred, *The Super Supervisor*, Positive Presentations, Inc., Greensboro, NC, 1986.

A hypocritical manager causes resentment that they may not realize.

Are You Responding Timely? You are a busy manager, so how do you find time to communicate confidently when you are stretched? There are ways! The more you engage in written, practiced communication, the more proficient you become. Only delay timely communication if you have a competing obligation that will not wait; just make sure it does not become a habit. Keep in mind, the longer you wait to communicate with an employee about an issue, the more difficult it becomes to declare its importance. They are apt to believe that if it was truly important, you would have addressed it quickly. If you schedule follow-up with an employee, make sure you get back with them when you say you will. If you find you have to change a meeting, let them know as soon as possible. Don't wait until the designated meeting time to tell them you need to postpone.

The longer you wait to communicate with an employee about an issue, the more difficult it becomes to declare its importance.

Are You Approaching Them with Respect? "I felt disrespected." Countless times, I have received this reply from employees in response to my question asking why they engaged in misconduct toward their manager. Before you engage an employee in a conversation that involves corrective action, even if it is just constructive criticism, you should ask yourself: "Am I approaching the employee with anger? Am I approaching the employee with ego? With frustration?" And so on. If it is anything other than an objective intention to correct the behavior, you should press pause. Likewise if you are being approached by an emotional employee, you should hold firm to your professional demeanor.

Early in my career, I felt a need to prove myself, so when I was confronted by an employee whose emotions were running high, I would respond in kind. It included shouting and I quickly learned it made me feel unprofessional. I learned to behave differently by modeling others who I respect. I remember watching a general manager admirably handle a difficult situation. I was sitting at his desk when the union president, George, stormed in angrily. Jim told him he was not going to listen unless George calmed down and talked to him with respect. There was a bit of back and forth between them and Jim never raised his voice, never changed his message. Finally he said, "Either change your tone or leave, and you are not welcome back in this office until you do." George blustered a bit and then was shown out of the office and he was not allowed back in until he was able to talk calmly. I learned from lessons like that; you don't have to be "showy" or loud in your engagements. I learned to divorce myself from the emotion and focus on the issue. It is hard for an engagement to escalate negatively when one person remains calm and respectful.

Are You Listening? At least once, you should hear the employee's side of the issue. For one, it is respectful and it will go a long way toward determining how the employee views you. It is also a way to learn whether there is more to a situation than meets the eye. What an employee says (and, in some instances, what they do not say) can be very significant. I recall having been visited in my office unexpectedly by a colleague during a very busy time. She walked in nonchalantly and said hello. I opened my mouth to let her know I was preoccupied and to ask if she could come back later. But she closed the door before sitting down and it gave me pause. She started off with light small-talk; I took a deep breath and decided to engage with her for a bit. It took just a few minutes for her to start talking about her life, including troubles involving a child on drugs. She started crying. She said things were spiraling out of control and she didn't know how she could go on. We agreed we would contact the company's employee assistance program (EAP) together and she was directed for help that same day. Had I not listened to the employee (nonverbal cues and verbal ones), I wouldn't have learned the seriousness of her situation and she might have gone home that day, feeling even more distraught.

Are You Prepared? If you have not documented and gathered evidence, then you are not prepared! If you have not imagined it, scripted it and practiced it as we discussed in trait #2 on page 96, then you are not prepared.

Are You Offering Encouragement? Offering encouragement is not a sign of weakness. It goes back to your intent — are you truly seeking to reach an agreeable solution? Even if you don't like the person, offer encouragement "as if you do," to quote another recommendation from Mildred Ramsey's book, *The Super Supervisor*.[12] One time, I was given the responsibility of having a conversation with an employee about improving her personal hygiene. To make matters worse, I did not care for the employee and I had no doubt the feeling was mutual. I scripted the message, practiced it, imagined her likely responses and prepared accordingly. I left all emotion out and, when the time came, the conversation went as well as I could have hoped. In the moment that mattered, when she looked me in the eye, she did not see condescension or ridicule. I stuck to the facts, gave her the opportunity to talk (she said it was a medical issue and she would talk with her doctor) and I encouraged her not to dwell on it. I assured her that only a couple of individuals knew we were having the conversation, so she could focus on what can be done

---

12 Ramsey, Mildred, *The Super Supervisor*, Positive Presentations, Inc., Greensboro, NC, 1986.

to address it and we could move along. We were never friends, but the civility of our relationship improved after that conversation.

Do You Have a Go-Forward Plan Documented and Signed?

A documented action plan may sound like overkill, but if you don't come away with written agreement on how you will work going forward, then you are setting the stage for unnecessary work down the road. Two popular quotes illustrate this very well:

- **"A goal without a plan is just a wish." (Antoine de Saint-Exupery)** Without accountability, the most well-intentioned employee will revert to the undesirable behavior. A plan helps the employee stay on track, setting them up to succeed; and

- **"If you didn't document it, it didn't happen." (every employment law attorney I have ever worked with)** It's an embarrassing and frustrating experience for managers to have important details of an agreement reduced to "he said, she said." But that is what often happens when you fail to document.

I recall working with a likeable manager who was preparing to counsel an employee regarding his attendance problem. The goal was to come away with a written action plan. Afterward, when the manager and I sat down to debrief, it seemed all had gone well until we reviewed the action plan. The first item was "the manager will call the employee if they haven't reported to work at least 15 minutes before the start of the shift" and so on. The manager had assumed over half of the responsibility! So we discussed how the action plan should outline how the *employee* will take ownership of their situation, and how the manager will support those efforts and what that might look like.

Are You Re-enforcing the Go-Forward Plan? One of the worst things you can do to your credibility as a manager is fail to follow through. When you don't follow through on your stated actions, you have told your employees what they can expect from you. You will not gain respect by going easy on poor performers; if you are fortunate, they will perform to the minimum acceptable level and not hold you over a barrel. Furthermore, your strong performers will eventually lose motivation and your department productivity and work environment will suffer. Be careful about making statements that you don't intend to follow up on or don't have the authority to enforce. Do what you say you will do, so that you will be known for being a person of your word.

One of the worst things you can do to your credibility as a manager is fail to follow through.

GO FORWARD CONFIDENTLY

The self-check list I shared on page 95 is based on conversations and learning over many years. Combined with effective training, it works to give managers the appropriate confidence to manage employee compliance with mutual respect while they work to adhere to company expectations. But I must be realistic — there is no silver bullet. No matter how respectful or effective you are as a leader, like my colleague Frank, you are still a target. And, of course, we are all human ... works in progress and prone to missteps. In my early career, a lot of the learnings came from my company's employment law attorney, Phil. He was a model for me and then an unofficial mentor after our formal working relationship ended. One of his philosophies was "make yourself a target out of range."[13] It resonated powerfully with me — first as a target myself and then as I worked with managers navigating the compliance-related landmines that come with employee relations. So, it became my philosophy too.

---

13 Lawson, Philip J., "Target Out of Range," Wimberly, Lawson, Wright, Daves & Jones PLLC, Knoxville, TN.

To quote Dr. Brené Brown, "I leaned into my discomfort at work" and owned that I am a target in my role.[14] It led me to imagine a workplace where I have communication skills that empower me to manage employee performance before they got out of my control. To handle myself with poise under difficult employee situations. Where I felt confident that I wasn't saying or doing something that would land me in legal trouble. And if I was named in a dispute (which I was), I was reassured I had done the necessary things to minimize my exposure and the company's exposure too. And now, as an HR contractor/consultant, I enjoy using these same tools outlined for you here in this book chapter to help my clients — typically busy CEOs and HR departments — to improve leadership skills and strengthen their cultures of compliance.

You too can learn to manage employees – every day – with both confidence and compliance. I encourage you not to delay. Be open to improving your communication skills. Use the self-check list to help you resolve issues. Practice using real-life examples. And make the imagined, ideal workplace a reality!

----

14   Brown, Brené, "If You Want Progress Create an Uncomfortable Environment," Inc.com.

ABOUT THE AUTHOR

Lisa M. Johnson
SHRM-SCP

Lisa M. Johnson is an internationally experienced human resources professional who has worked with leaders from numerous industries in the public and private sectors. Her training style and insights have been successfully applied in organizations and settings of varying sizes and cultures. She is skilled in group facilitation, keynote speaking and individual coaching.

Lisa has more than 25 years of proven experience as a human resources generalist, with a background that spans from global project management, to change management, to labor relations. Today, her focus reflects the intersection of leadership development and compliance awareness. As founder and owner of HR Know-How LLC, she enjoys helping busy CEOs and HR professionals develop their leaders, and believes that bringing humanity and consistency to their interactions is key to personal growth and organizational productivity.

Lisa earned a Bachelor's in personnel/industrial relations from the University of Kentucky and an MBA from Lewis University. In addition to holding certifications for coaching and training, she is also a Society for Human Resource Management Senior Certified Professional (SHRM-SCP). She is an adjunct instructor for Workforce Solutions, a customized training arm of the Kentucky Community & Technical College system.

Lisa is a member of the National Speakers Association – KY chapter, and the Society for Human Resource Management – Louisville chapter, where she serves in the role of Legislative Chair. She resides in Bardstown, Kentucky, where she is a proud member of the Bardstown-Nelson County Chamber of Commerce.

Learn more and contact Lisa:

✉ Lisa@HRKnowHow.org

🌐 HRKnowHow.org

⬛ Facebook.com/HRKnowHowLLC

⬛ LinkedIn.com/in/HRKnowHow

🐦 Twitter.com/HRKnowHow

⬛ Instagram.com/HRKnowHow

📞 502-709-0199

Chapter five

MICHAEL RIDER

"Living an Engaged Life at Work Through Mentoring"

When I sat down to write this book chapter, I had just celebrated eight months of sobriety. In the previous 12 months, I left an employer; realized I was severely alcoholic; lost a marriage (including three step-sons I loved but was unequipped to love well); relocated; started a business; lost my mind; entered recovery; battled the darkness of addiction, depression, financial ruin and loneliness; found hope and faith that work; and had just begun learning how to live life. Again, but for the first time.

We spend more of our waking life at work than anywhere else. So what better place to feel accepted, acknowledged and seen?

And it's all gotten me thinking — about what it is to be balanced, healthy, happy, safe, engaged. We spend more of our waking life at work than anywhere else. So what better place to feel accepted, acknowledged and seen? Our workplaces are where we are often our most vulnerable, our most incredible, and our most full of potential. But it doesn't take a string of personal crises for you to recognize that many workplaces — maybe even *most* workplaces — are coming up short when it comes to building cultures of trust and support. The vast majority of us would never share with their boss or colleagues what I shared in the opening paragraph of this chapter, for fear of judgment, retribution, gossip or even job loss. And I believe that's because the vast majority of people working in American companies don't have a true mentor they can trust.

THE CASE FOR MENTORING AS A BUSINESS CATALYST

Imagine ... a workplace where you feel you belong.

Imagine ... a workplace where your values are aligned with the organization's values, and where organizational values are lived each day through business decisions and interpersonal relations.

Imagine ... a workplace where your colleagues — up, down and across the organization — know your personal and professional goals and dreams, *and* help you obtain them.

In the past week, how many hours did you spend at work (in an office or a factory or a restaurant, for example), or conducting work-related activities for your employer? 40? 50? More? If you're like most people, you're spending a quarter of your time (or more!) "on the job," serving an organization and its leadership the very best you can. Wouldn't it be great if you looked forward to spending time at that place each day, and if you were prepared to give it your all because the company gave so much to you? Imagine feeling fulfilled at the end of a day's work, and even grateful and energized at the close of each week.

This is the workplace that I imagine, in which each employee is valued, customers sing, and organizational outcomes are maximized. And I believe it is possible. Getting there requires building an engagement strategy using mentoring as a catalyst. When every employee in an organization is given the chance to be both a mentor and a mentee — to learn and to inspire each day — we can go beyond fit and skill, and dive deeper into dreams. And dreams make everything possible, for individuals, teams and entire organizations. Supportive, engaging workplace cultures create not just personal results but organizational results too — including profitable growth, employee retention and brand value.

When every employee in an organization is given the chance to be both a mentor and a mentee — to learn and to inspire each day — we can go beyond fit and skill, and dive deeper into dreams.

ENGAGEMENT: A NOBLE GOAL AND AN ORGANIZATIONAL SECRET WEAPON

It wasn't that long ago that I was in a job where I wasn't engaged. I felt like an oddball, disconnected and fearful. The management team's commitment to employees seemed one-sided, and employees were not nurtured to achieve success but managed with a "sink or swim" mentality. It was disheartening, to say the least. The only organizational "mission and purpose" I knew about? The leaders' collective desire to "hit the numbers." *Yuck*. Sound motivating to you? Well, it wasn't. It was hard to get excited about going to work each day, and when I left employment there at the two-year mark, I felt exhausted and frustrated. Not just for myself but for the company, my co-workers and our clients.

The organization's failure to fully engage their employees resulted in a lose-lose-lose situation for all involved.

Many of you reading this book, sadly, may have stories of your own about jobs you've done where you were underappreciated and less than engaged. Think back to those experiences (or reflect on your current situation if it's suboptimal), then think about what it would take to "fix" it. Ponder for just a minute on how different it is when you're *engaged* in your work. You have energy for the work; you wake up looking forward to contributing; you feel a part of the organization; you exude a passion for the company. Excitement. Camaraderie. Value. Purpose. Growth!

Ponder for just a minute on how different it is when you're *engaged* in your work. You have energy for the work; you wake up looking forward to contributing; you feel a part of the organization; you exude a passion for the company. Excitement. Camaraderie. Value. Purpose. Growth!

By now, you won't be surprised to learn that I've always been passionate about workplace mentoring. And after having experienced some of life's biggest proverbial "ups and downs," I'm more committed than ever to being a great mentor to others, seeking great mentors for myself, and inspiring decision-makers (at any organization that will listen!) to invest in mentor-driven engagement strategies.

Before your company is likely to implement or improve a meaningful mentorship program, though, someone at the top of the organization must be as passionate about mentoring as I am. That's why I'm a big fan of Nikki Lewallen's *Gut + Science* podcast, which focuses its episodes on interviewing top CEOs about how they create and nurture people-first cultures. Culture is, for better or for worse, inspired by attitudes and behaviors at the top. No stranger to the important role that the CEO plays (Lewallen is CEO of the business development firm Rainmakers), she is an expert in the interplay between mentoring, engagement and culture.

I was recently struck by something Lewallen said on the air and on her website: "People-first leaders should be asking this overarching question, 'What are you doing to ensure your employees find meaning in the work they do?' But first, how do *they* define 'meaning?'"[1]

Whether you own the company, lead from the C-suite, manage a small team or informally mentor just one person in your organization, you have the opportunity to be a "people-first leader." I believe it starts with Lewallen's call to action. Do you know how your people define "meaning?" Have you ever asked them? Likewise, have you ever taken the time to talk to your boss about what makes work meaningful to you, and how the job and the surrounding culture are matching up to your hopes?

Whether you own the company, lead from the C-suite, manage a small team or informally mentor just one person in your organization, you have the opportunity to be a "people-first leader."

Do this: Next time you have a scheduled touch-base meeting with one of your employees or mentees, clear the agenda to focus on just one topic. Ask Nikki Lewallen's question. Find out how your employee or mentee defines meaning in their work and career, and seek to truly understand. Listen closely, and be sure to say "tell me more" when the conversation takes a pause. Then find out if the work and the culture at your organization are viewed through the mentee or employee's own "meaning"

------

1   Lewallen, Nikki, "Share the Love in the Workplace," Episode 042, Gut+Science Podcast, Feb. 14, 2019, https://gutplusscience.com/valentines-2019/.

filter. Can you do something different (and can they make changes too) to better align their daily work with what is meaningful to them, and do so in a way that still focuses their talents on what the company needs from them? I promise you that this could be the most important 30-60 minutes you've ever spent together.

This simple exercise is just one way for you to see, in action, how one-on-one mentoring (formally or informally) can create employee engagement that ignites productive relationships and results at work. But before we dig further into what a "mentoring program" looks like, and how they work, let's continue to explore the importance of employee engagement, shall we?

"Employee engagement" is more than a modern business buzzword. It's an organizational secret weapon or superpower, if you know how to create it, keep it and wield it. So what *is* employee engagement? Investopedia defines it as "a business management concept that describes the level of enthusiasm and dedication a worker feels toward his/her job. Engaged employees care about their work and about the performance of the company and feel that their efforts make a difference."2 For our purposes here, I think this is a pretty good definition around which to frame our conversation. If you're paying attention at work, you can easily see who is engaged and who is disengaged. And if your company is anything like other American companies, you might be shocked by what you see. In their oft-cited work conducted a few years ago, Gallup discovered that 70% of U.S. workers are either not engaged or actively disengaged on a daily basis.3 It's time you did something about it.

---

2   Investopedia, "Employee Engagement," https://www.investopedia.com/terms/e/employee-engagement.asp.

3   Sorenson, Susan, and Garman, Keri. "How to Tackle U.S. Employees' Stagnating Engagement," *Gallup Business Journal,* June 11, 2013, https://news.gallup.com/businessjournal/162953/tackle-employees-stagnating-engagement.aspx.

Engagement is not about workplaces full of rainbows and unicorns.
It's not about generous perks or big salaries or lenient bosses. "Employee
engagement does not mean employee *happiness*," explains author and
thought leader Kevin Kruse [emphasis mine]. He also contends that
it's not employee satisfaction either. "Employee engagement is the
emotional commitment the employee has to the organization and its
goals. This emotional commitment means engaged employees actually care about their work and their company. They don't work just for
a paycheck, or just for the next promotion, but work on behalf of the
organization's goals. When employees care — when they are *engaged* —
they use discretionary effort."4

And when entire teams or companies give a little extra to their work
because they're engaged, the results show up on the bottom line.
Remember, we're not talking rainbows and unicorns here. A global study
conducted by Towers Perrins in 2007 revealed striking data about the
relationship between employee engagement and financial performance.
"A study of 40 global companies which involved a regression analysis
of company financial results against engagement data ... found that
firms with the highest percentage of engaged employees collectively
increased operating income 19% and earnings per share 28% year to
year. Those companies with the lowest percentage of engaged employees
showed year-to-year declines of 33% in operating income and 11% in
earnings per share."5

---

4   Kruse, Kevin, "What is Employee Engagement and Why?," *Forbes*,
    June 22, 2012, https://www.forbes.com/sites/kevinkruse/2012/06/22/
    employee-engagement-what-and-why/#477633877f37.

5   Towers Perrins, "Towers Perrins Study Finds Significant
    'Engagement Gap" Among Global Workforce," Oct. 22, 2007,
    https://www.businesswire.com/news/home/20071021005052/en/
    Towers-Perrin-Study-Finds-Significant-Engagement-Gap.

Have I got your attention yet? Indeed, money talks. It's hard not to imagine what our respective companies could have accomplished — for our stakeholders and our employees — this past year with a 19% increase in operating income. Conversely, it's irresponsible for us to disregard the cost of disengagement. Based on its research, McLean & Company asserts that "a disengaged employee costs an organization approximately $3,400 for every $10,000 in annual salary."[6] What are you paying your employees, and what are they costing you in return?

MENTORING AS THE SUPERHIGHWAY TO ENGAGEMENT

Clearly, engagement matters. So how do organizations and their leaders create this kind of magic? By launching and maintaining the kind of organizational change that conveys an ambitious vison and a people-centric set of values.

Clearly, engagement matters. So how do organizations and their leaders create this kind of magic? By launching and maintaining the kind of organizational change that conveys an ambitious vison and a people-centric set of values. I believe that workplace mentoring programs should be a cornerstone in the foundation of this kind of supportive work environment where employees connect and thrive.

What is mentoring? Mentoring is different from managing. Managing's first priority is to get the job done. Mentoring is putting the developmental needs of the mentee first. So, while most managers

---

6   Warner, Justin, "Show Me the Money: The ROI of Employee Engagement," DecisionWise, July 10, 2018, https://www.decision-wise.com/show-me-the-money-the-roi-of-employee-engagement/.

can and do *supervise*, they don't always mentor. Managers usually tell the employee what to do; mentors rarely direct their mentees, but rather, ask questions to help their mentee discover the solution.

Mentoring is about listening to the needs of the individual; it is about asking questions. It is also about sharing experiences so that others can learn from those stories.

MENTORING PROGRAMS

Many Fortune 500 companies have long understood the value of mentoring strategies. In fact, it's been reported that more than 71% of Fortune 500 companies offering mentoring programs.[7]

However, the challenge is that small and mid-sized companies often lack the resources to offer mentoring programs. Mentoring strategies can be expensive and difficult to administer, causing smaller organizations to shy away from this strategy, and to simply assume that supervisors are doing well enough to be "mentors" during daily interactions or regular touch-base meetings with their employees. They might believe that mentoring should happen organically, and happen when employees seek support from those in leadership, and those in leadership reach down to help grow talent internally. This wishful (and faulty) thinking happens in organizations of all sizes, but especially in smaller ones.

The truth of the matter is that few mentoring strategies happen "naturally." Employees may lack the self-awareness or confidence to ask for help, and leaders may be unaware of the needs of those in the trenches.

---

7   Silard Kantor, Julie, and Crosser, A., "Four Key Benefits of Workplace Mentoring Initiatives," *HuffPost*, March 11, 2016, https://www.huffpost.com/entry/four-key-benefits-of-work_b_9432716.

THE VALUE OF EXTERNAL MENTORING

The good news for small and mid-sized organizations that value the benefits of mentoring to aid engagement is that they can achieve these benefits by working with external mentoring programs. Working with a firm that administers external mentoring programs can have lower start-up costs and faster implementation than building something in-house. And while there are many great mentoring programs with national acclaim (like Wisdom Share or Menttium) and other programs that specialize in working with niche groups (like particular industries, professions or even genders), I have a vested interested in and love for one such firm exploding in this space: Engage Mentoring. I currently serve in the role of Ambassador for Engage Mentoring in Louisville, KY. The program is powered by Diverse Talent Strategies in Indianapolis and operates on a simple but proven methodology that hinges on a mix of leadership development, corporate social responsibility and HR data to help drive organizational results and build sustainable company cultures.

Partnering with a firm that offers external mentoring programs offers many benefits, including the possibility that your employees will thrive under the mentorship of outside professionals who have no vested interest in your company or its possibly biased and outmoded ways of operating. Fresh perspectives can spark outstanding results. One of the things I personally value about an external mentoring partner like Engage Mentoring is the structure they can provide. Workplace mentoring programs tend to be loose, informal and inconsistent in what they offer one employee over the next. Engage Mentoring, on the other hand, provides structure for the entire process — from meeting agendas to meeting schedules to communications templates to help participants get introduced and started collaborating. External mentoring firms can also hold you accountable by helping you track the outcomes of your mentoring efforts. And if you're hesitating about external programs that match employees with mentors, ask yourself: Knowing that the vast majority of new couples in the U.S. today are meeting online (often through dating services that "match" them with suitable mates), isn't it time to broaden the field for workplace mentoring relationships too?

MENTORING MODELS

As you can see, mentoring programs can be administered in different ways. There are also many mentoring models to consider. Just remember that no matter how you go about building and maintaining your mentorship program, it's crucial to be consistent on strategy.

Excellent mentoring strategies have four elements:

1.   Training for both mentors and mentees
2.   Defined program structure
3.   Systems to match skills and dreams
4.   Data and reporting

Training for both mentors and mentees. Leaders don't become excellent mentors by osmosis; they become mentors through training. Similarly, mentors don't understand how to benefit from these strategies until they receive training.

_____

Leaders don't become excellent mentors by osmosis; they become mentors through training.

_____

Employees want to be involved. But how do they maximize their involvement? How does the employee do a good job as a mentee?

Training is necessary not just at the onset of the program, but throughout. Training helps set expectations, roles and accountabilities.

It helps participants to feel a sense of clarity about the purpose of the program, and to understand that they are not alone in this journey (and that being mentored is not a remediation tactic for poor performers, nor is it a punishment for mentors).

Mentors must learn skills around inquiry and listening. They need to understand how to hold their protégés accountable. And, they need to understand the program structure.

Mentees need to learn about being open to feedback, being coachable and being teachable. They may need help in learning how to ask for specific help. They also may need to anticipate their needs and proactively ask for help and assistance.

Defined program structure. Some companies begin mentoring programs with strong initial results, but often these programs are unsustainable because they don't have the infrastructure to sustain success. With a defined program, mentors and mentees understand how often they should meet, what they should discuss, and how the accountability for the program is managed. Consider having templates for conversations, worksheets and activities to help kickstart conversations. Before the relationship can take on its own natural dynamics, it will likely need some structure to give the participants guiderails and some contexts in which to think, feel and thrive.

Systems to match skills and dreams. Many mentoring programs focus only on skills, such as how to be more successful at cold calling, how to be an effective speaker, or how to be more effective in delegating. And these may be critically important competencies for you or your employees. But what makes mentoring effective in spurring employee engagement is focusing on employee dreams. Dreams fall flat far too often and when they do, we lose. We lose, our families and friends lose, and our employers and communities lose.

What makes mentoring effective in spurring employee engagement is focusing on employee dreams. Dreams fall flat far too often and when they do, we lose. We lose, our families and friends lose, and our employers and communities lose.

Ask yourself "why" you are doing the work of building or maintaining relationships at work, and even implementing a formal mentoring program. The possibility that you might restore and make possible other peoples' dreams is a huge "why" to inspire what we are doing!

If organizations can demonstrate that they care about the employees' dreams, then they can capture their enthusiasm and passion.

Data and reporting. Data tells a story. Without organizational stories, it is difficult — if not impossible — to define organizational results. Has turnover been reduced? Are engagement scores higher? Is productivity up? Can the organization more easily attract and retain the talent that it needs?

By building in pre- and post-program surveys and ongoing assessment tools, organizations can measure and track the success of their mentoring strategies and determine the return on investment.

Data in the HR space is huge today. You should collect employee feedback data, at minimum, quarterly and take an agile approach to reviewing the data and implementing changes based on facts, not gut. Companies who take this kind of agile approach will typically see a 23% reduction in turnover year one and about 20% increase in team performance.[8]

---

8   Lewallen, Nikki, personal conversation, March 2019.

MENTORING IN ACTION

At the end of the day, mentoring is about the people on both sides of the relationship — about what they need, what they deserve, and what they can share and learn. For me, having a mentor and being a mentor continues to improve my life in every way — in business; in now being a single, divorced dad to a beautiful 5-year-old daughter; in recovery from alcoholism; and as a person learning how to better navigate life's up and downs. I have "done life" for decades without having the right people in place to gain experience from, and to share wisdom and struggles with. And I can tell you, a mentorless life doesn't work. Being engaged with mentors and mentees provides the tools, directions and inspiration to be "a part of" instead of "apart from."

Being engaged with mentors and mentees provides the tools, directions and inspiration to be "a part of" instead of "apart from."

Just as companies that think of strategic planning as a one-time activity are doomed to fail, those that think of mentoring as a flavor-of-the-day HR trend are paying lip service to their employees. Mentoring — like all fundamental elements of corporate culture — should be a way of life, with no defined end point at which leaders dust off their hands and say "Well, that initiative is complete. Next!" Employees deserve our thoughtful attention to how we engage them through mentoring. If we want them to stay more than a few years (the average job tenure in the U.S. today),9 we need to be doing more to earn their loyalty, passion and discretionary effort. Mentoring is a great place to start.

---

9   Bureau of Labor Statistics, United States Department of Labor, "Employee Tenure Summary," Sept. 20, 2018, https://www.bls.gov/news.release/tenure.nr0.htm.

Getting better and *being* better — in work and in life — are complex endeavors. I have learned, through addiction recovery and through workplace mentoring — two experiences that may seem unrelated to some readers — that bringing our best selves (to work and to the world) requires self-direction and active support. Just as I cannot imagine thriving in my life of sobriety without support networks and mentors, as well as compassionate and trusted colleagues and loved ones, none of us can imagine thriving at work without similar ecosystems built on mutual respect and a genuine desire to help each other be better. There is perhaps nowhere you spend more time than at your workplace. It's the perfect place to be seen, understood, respected and listened to. And cultures that do precisely *that* are built deliberately ... by leaders who care.

By leaders like you.

ABOUT THE AUTHOR

Michael Rider

Michael Rider is a talented and respected sales and marketing leader whose distinguished career working for turnaround and high-growth organizations has led him to be sought-after for his valuable insights about what works when stakes are high. He has extensive expertise in client needs analysis with a consultative approach to sales in cutting-edge tech, insurance, and benefits-design industries. Michael is the founder of Rider Risk Management Services, LLC, where he works with the C-suite, helping them to realign their operations to their mission and vision by focusing on people, technology and benefits to reduce costs, drive engagement, streamline processes and increase ROI.

Michael is committed to being an attuned listener, persuasive presenter, worthy collaborator and negotiator, and passionate connector. He prides himself on being able to forge solid relationships with strategic partners, build consensus across multiple organizational levels, and drive improved outcomes utilizing people, strategy, KPIs and budgets.

Michael is passionate about giving back to people, the community and businesses through championing mentoring, being a megaphone and embracing the spirit of servant leadership. He is the 2019 Chair of Sponsor Fundraising for the Louisville Society for Human Resource Management (LSHRM). Michael studied business at Western Kentucky University and Clark College, and currently lives and works in Louisville, Kentucky. This is his first book.

Learn more and contact Michael:

- LinkedIn.com/in/Michael-Rider
- Twitter.com/Rider_Michael
- Facebook.com/Rider.Michael.E
- Instagram.com/Rider.Michael.E

@work SERIES

ABOUT THE @WORK SERIES AND ITS CREATORS

The @Work Series of professional anthologies was the brainchild of book strategist and HR expert Cathy Fyock, who knew that human resources and organizational development experts had so much to offer to the business marketplace when it came to contemporary insights about what makes companies tick. She also knew that busy HR and OD professionals often found themselves pressed for the time to solo-author a book, and that they're inherently collaborative. Bringing such professionals together to co-author an anthology made perfect sense!

The first book in the series was *Humans@Work*, published in 2017 by Red Letter Publishing (a company whose book assets would later be acquired by Silver Tree Publishing). On the heels of the success of *Humans@Work*, Cathy assembled more teams of brilliant leaders to write *Compassion@Work* (2017), *You@Work* (2018), and finally *Imagination@Work* (2019). Several of the anthology authors featured in this series have gone on to publish solo-authored books.

And the story of how Cathy met Silver Tree Publishing founder Kate Colbert is just proof that books are magical, and that they bring people together. Cathy and Kate met in 2014 in New York, on an airport shuttle to an NSA-sponsored conference about book authorship and publishing success. Three years later, they began collaborating on the anthology series, as well as many other books. It was meant to be!

This book is the last book of the @Work Series, but just the beginning of what is possible when experienced and accomplished business professionals come together to share their tips, tricks, stories, methods and insights.

Learn more about Cathy Fyock LLC and Silver Tree Publishing on the following pages. We hope you've enjoyed this book, and that you'll keep in touch!

SILVER TREE PUBLISHING

Silver Tree Publishing has been proud to present the @Work Series of professional anthologies. The four books in this series — *Humans@Work, Compassion@Work, You@Work* and *Imagination@Work* — are available from Amazon and through special arrangements with the authors. Full of practical and inspiring solutions for common workplace challenges, these books are the perfect gifts for seasoned and aspiring leaders.

Silver Tree Publishing is home to several publishing imprints:

SILVER TREE PUBLISHING

Our flagship imprint for nonfiction business books

Silver Linings MEDIA

Our newest imprint, dedicated to memoirs and inspiring biographies

Sterling Forest PRESS

Our literary imprint for creative writers

Keep in Touch and Learn More!

To learn more about publishing your book through Silver Tree — a unique collaborative publisher for serious authors who value a lasting partnership and a high-quality book — visit SilverTreePublishing.com and follow us on social media.

Your Brand, Our Books ... a Magical Combination

Ask us about creating custom-branded editions of our books for your upcoming professional conferences or for your company's stakeholders, complete with the opportunity for your leader to write a foreword for your limited-edition books.

Silver Tree Publishing is the sister company of Silver Tree Market Research and Silver Tree Communications, all founded and led by acclaimed author and marketer Kate Colbert.

SILVER TREE Market Research

SILVER TREE Communications

SilverTreeMarketResearch.com | KateColbert.com

DO YOU DREAM ABOUT WRITING YOUR BOOK?

Do you dream of writing your own book to establish credibility, document your thought leadership, and further your career? If so, then call on Cathy Fyock — The Business Book Strategist!

Whether you think you don't have the time to write your book, are confused about how to get started, or are not sure how to get your book across the finish line, Cathy can help. Since 2014, she's helped more than 150 professionals become published authors.

Cathy has created a unique community of authors and aspiring authors, and helps authors leverage their books to accelerate their businesses and amplify their messages.

Cathy's One-on-One Coaching includes the following:

Cathy Fyock
The Business Book Strategist

- A customized strategy session with Cathy at the beginning of the process, where she and the author get clarity on the purpose, thesis, target reader, structure/outline, and project plan

- One-on-one calls scheduled regularly

- Unlimited email and telephone support

- Cathy's online program, delivered in six modules, covering your goals for your book, obstacles and strategies to overcome them, preparation tactics, creating your plan, and getting it completed

- Copies of three of Cathy's books — *On Your Mark*, *Blog2Book*, and *The Speaker Author* — plus her monthly newsletter

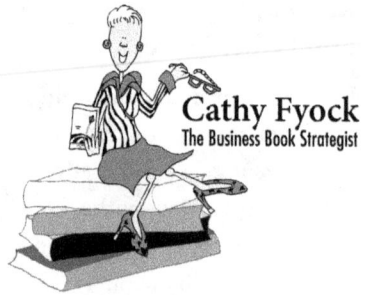

- Group coaching calls twice each month, featuring celebrations, writing prompts, focused questions, and meaty content (recorded if you can't attend live)

- Bonus Master Class monthly on writing, publishing, or marketing your book

- Ability to move to Cathy's Author Mastermind Group once your manuscript is at 80% completion, so that you can learn best practices and gain support from your author colleagues

Cathy believes that, as authors, we change the world one word at a time. Become part of her community by scheduling a complimentary strategy session today. Simply send an email to Cathy@CathyFyock.com with "Strategy" in the subject line.

ON YOUR MARK
FROM FIRST WORD TO FIRST DRAFT IN SIX WEEKS
CATHY FYOCK AND KEVIN WILLIAMSON

BLOG 2 BOOK
CATHY FYOCK

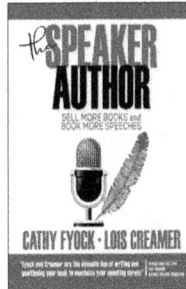

the SPEAKER AUTHOR
SELL MORE BOOKS and BOOK MORE SPEECHES
CATHY FYOCK · LOIS CREAMER

www.ingramcontent.com/pod-product-compliance
Lightning Source LLC
Chambersburg PA
CBHW052137270326
41930CB00012B/2920